Tapestry 3

Ontario Edition

Les Asselstine

Rod Peturson

Wendy Dubois

Norma Luks

Judy Morrison

Bob Shields

 **Harcourt**
Canada

Harcourt Canada

Toronto Orlando San Diego London Sydney

Canadian Cataloguing in Publication Data
Main entry under title:

Tapestry 3

ISBN 0-7747-0585-X

1. Social sciences — Juvenile literature.
I. Asselstine, Les, 1943-

H95.T363 2000   300   C99-932708-9

Les Asselstine
formerly Waterloo County Board of Education, Ontario

Rod Peturson
Windsor Board of Education, Ontario

Norma Luks
formerly York Region Board of Education, Ontario

Wendy Dubois
Burnaby School District, British Columbia

Judy Morrison
Burnaby School District, British Columbia

Bob Shields
School of Education, Acadia University, Nova Scotia

Cover
A farm near Newcastle, Ontario

Reviewers
Walter Baslyk
Protestant School Board of Greater Montreal, Quebec
Roland Case
Simon Fraser University, British Columbia
Walter G. Donovan
OISE/University of Toronto, Ontario
Eldon Jamieson
Eastern School District, Prince Edward Island
Judith Laskin
Toronto District School Board, Ontario
Dr. Keith W. Ludlow
Vinland/Strait of Belle Isle Integrated School District, Newfoundland
Ken MacInnis
Halifax Regional School Board, Nova Scotia
Kim Newlove
Saskatoon Board of Education, Saskatchewan
May Peiluck
Evergreen School Division 22, Manitoba
Mary K. Romanko
Edmonton School District 7, Alberta
Carol Ward
School District 17, New Brunswick

Bias Reviewers
Ourlaine Pashley
Toronto District School Board, Ontario
Shauneen Pete-Willet
Saskatoon Board of Education, Saskatchewan

Writers/Editors: Laura Edlund, Mary Knittl, Ian Nussbaum, Brett Savory
Senior Production Editor: Karin Fediw
Production Coordinator: Tanya Mossa
Production Assistant: Jennifer Smiley
Photo Researcher: Mary Rose MacLachlan
Interior Design and Layout: Andrew Smith Graphics/ FIZZZ Design Inc.
Cover Design: Mighty Design
Cover Image: D. Roitner/Canada in Stock/Ivy Images
Back Cover Images (left to right): Beedell/Canada in Stock, Deborah Crowle, Suzanne Mogensen, Patty Gallinger

 This book is printed in Canada on acid-free paper.

1 2 3 4 5   04 03 02 01 00

ISLANDS

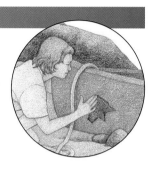

CELEBRATIONS

Generations

INFORMATION STATION

To find out more, look in the Information Station at the end of this book.

ISLANDS

Although islands come in many shapes and sizes, all islands have two things in common—they are surrounded by water and they are constantly changing. Find out about islands and island life in Canada and throughout the world. Discover how some islands have been changed by nature and people and how people live on different islands.

WASHED ASHORE

What would it be like to be stranded on a desert island?
How would you cope if you had to rely on only yourself
and your surroundings to survive?

Imagine that you are canoeing with your brother or sister on a lake on a hot, windy summer day. You paddle to a distant part of the lake to explore a bay with a lot of little islands. You can no longer see the mainland as you travel among the islands.

Suddenly your boat hits a rock and overturns. Unhurt, you and your brother or sister swim to the canoe, turn it upright, and discover that the rock has torn a large hole in the bottom of the canoe. The two of you hold on to the canoe's side and slowly push it to the nearby rocky beach.

Once you have pulled your canoe onto the beach, you spread out the contents of your backpack to dry. You decide to take a look around. Before long you realize that you are stranded on a desert island. You and your brother or sister need to make some decisions as it may be some time before you are rescued. What can you eat and drink? Where can you sleep? What can you use for shelter? What can you do to keep busy? How can you let rescuers know where you are?

To Do

In this activity you are going to make decisions about how to survive on a desert island.

1. With a partner, examine the illustration on pages 8 to 9. Make a list of items that you can use to survive on the island. On your list, include
   - items that you brought to the island
   - items that are part of the island's natural setting

2. On your list, underline the five items you will need the most. Write down beside each item how you will use it. Can you use some items for more than one purpose?

3. Show how important you think each item is by numbering them from 1 (most important) to 5 (least important).

4. Compare your choices and the reasons for choosing these items with another pair of classmates.

5. Choose one of these activities to show what might happen during a three-day stay on the island:
   - Write a morning and an evening diary entry for each day on the island.
   - Write a log describing your daily routine.
   - Draw a comic strip of your daily routine.
   - Dramatize one event from each day.
   - Tape a conversation between you and your brother or sister.

Share your finished work with your classmates.

Tech Tools

You may wish to conduct a survey of the class to find out how many students chose each item in the picture as one of their five most important items for survival. Tally the results and make a graph to share the information. You can use a computer spreadsheet program to create this graph.

If Once You Have Slept on an Island

by Rachel Field

As you read this poem about staying on an island, think about how it compares to your own experience.

If once you have slept on an island
    You'll never be quite the same;
You may look as you looked the day before
    And go by the same old name,

You may bustle about in street and shop;
    You may sit at home and sew,
But you'll see blue water and wheeling gulls
    Wherever your feet may go.

You may chat with the neighbours of this and that
    And close to your fire keep,
But you'll hear ship whistle and lighthouse bell
    And tides beat through your sleep.

Oh, you won't know why, and you can't say how
    Such change upon you came,
But—once you have slept on an island
    You'll never be quite the same!

How did staying on the island change you? How did you change the island? If you could go back to the island, what would you do differently?

CANADIAN ISLANDS

One centimetre on this map is the same as 200 kilometres on the ground.

0   200   400   600
kilometres

ARCTIC OCEAN

Alaska

There are many islands in Canada. They are found in rivers and lakes, and in the oceans on the west, east, and north coasts. With so many islands in Canada, it is not surprising that a lot of people live on islands. The rest of the people live on the mainland—the biggest part of Canada. If you could live on any island in Canada, which one would you choose?

Yukon Territory

Northwest Territories

3

C A

5

British Columbia

Alberta

Saskatchewan

4

PACIFIC OCEAN

Queen Charlotte Islands

FOR YOUR INFORMATION

Manitoulin Island, in Lake Huron, is the largest island in a freshwater lake in the world. It is so large that it has more than 100 lakes of its own.

Victoria Island

Newfoundland

Manitoulin Island

Nunavut

A D A

Hudson Bay

Québec

Newfoundland

itoba

Ontario

New Brunswick

Nova Scotia

P.E.I.

Gulf of St. Lawrence

Lake Superior

Lake Michigan

Lake Huron

Lake Ontario

Lake Erie

ATLANTIC OCEAN

N
W   E
S

1

2

6

7

8

9

10

In this activity you are going to examine maps to find answers to these questions about Canadian islands.

1. Use the map on pages 12 to 13 and an atlas to answer these questions about islands in **Canada:**
   a) What does the map tell you about Canada?
   b) What does the map tell you about islands in Canada?
   c) Which Canadian island is closest to where you live?
   d) What are the names of the 10 Canadian islands marked on the map?
   e) Why does the map not show all of the islands in Canada?
   f) Which Canadian island is farthest north?
   g) Which Canadian island is farthest south?
   h) Which Canadian island is the largest?
   i) On which islands do you think people live? Why?

2. Use the map on pages 12 to 13 to answer these questions about **Vancouver Island, Prince Edward Island,** and **Baffin Island:**
   a) In what part of Canada is each island located?
   b) Which body of water surrounds each island?
   c) Which island is a province?
   d) In which province or territory are the other two islands located?
   e) Which island is longest? Which island is widest? How can you find out?
   f) How many times can the length of the shortest island fit into the length of the longest island?
   g) If you took the shortest path within Canada, which provinces would you go through to get from Prince Edward Island to Vancouver Island? How far would you travel?
   h) If two planes travelling at the same speed left Vancouver Island and Prince Edward Island at the same time, which one would arrive on Baffin Island first? How can you find out?

Share your answers with each other.

How To

Measure Distances Using a Line Scale

Line scales are used to show the real distances represented on maps. This line scale shows you that the distance between Town A and Town B is 500 km.

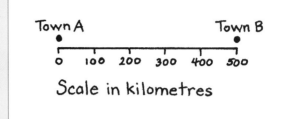

These steps explain one way to measure distances on a map using a line scale.

- Make a paper scale ruler by copying the line scale from the map onto the edge of a piece of paper.

- To measure the distance between Town A and Town C, place the 0 at one end of the distance you want to measure (Town A) and read the number at the other end of the distance (Town C).

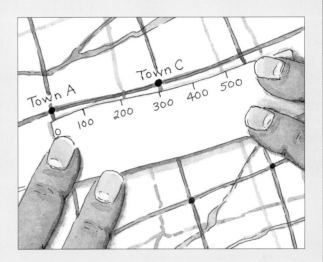

- If the distance you are measuring is longer than the line scale, make a longer scale ruler. Place your paper scale ruler under the line scale on the map so that the 500 km mark on your scale ruler is under the 0 of the line scale. Add more numbers to your scale ruler.

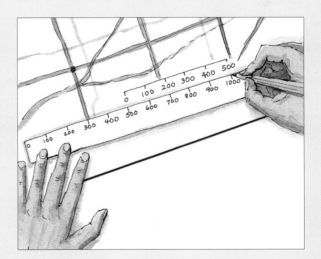

Many Places, Many Faces

If you were washed ashore on Vancouver Island on Canada's west coast, you would have lots of things to see and do! Vancouver Island's rich variety of physical features and natural resources—lakes, rivers, mountains, forests, and the Pacific Ocean—has given people many choices of where and how to live on this island.

Steven, Sara, and Krista live in different communities on Vancouver Island. Steven lives in Tofino, Sara lives in Campbell River, and Krista lives in Duncan. As you read their stories on pages 18 to 23, think about their lives. In what ways are their lives affected by their surroundings? How are their lives similar to and different from each other?

A **natural resource** is anything in nature that people find useful. Some natural resources, like forests, are **renewable** because they can be replaced or replace themselves.

Other natural resources, like oil or gas, are **non-renewable** because they cannot be replaced or replace themselves.

All resources should be used carefully—even renewable resources can be used faster than they can be replaced.

STRAIT

SAYWARD

HIGHWAY 19

VANCOUVER ISLAND

GOLD RIVER

CAMPBELL RIVER

Hwy. 28

STRATHCONA PARK

STRAIT OF GEORGIA

B.C. FERRIES

Hwy. 4

CLAYOQUOT SOUND

PORT ALBERNI

NANAIMO

TOFINO

UCLUELET

COWICHAN LAKE

PACIFIC RIM NATIONAL PARK

PORT RENFREW

Hwy. 1

DUNCAN

JUAN DE FUCA STRAIT

VICTORIA

Fishing is one of many jobs for people in Tofino.

Living in Tofino

Name

Steven Thompson, age 10

Community

Steven lives in **Tofino**, a small fishing village on the southern edge of **Clayoquot Sound**. His town is a popular tourist community for visitors to the **Pacific Rim National Park**. During the summer, thousands of tourists come to explore the rugged west coast of the island and to stay in its many campgrounds and lodges. In the winter, Tofino is a quiet community with a population of fewer than 1000 people. Tourism has created many jobs in the area, but some people worry that too many visitors may have a bad effect on the natural environment. To solve this problem, the government has made rules about the number of people who can hike or camp in the area.

People come from many places to hike on Vancouver Island's West Coast Trail.

Family

Steven lives with his father, George, and his older brother, Greg. They live in a three-bedroom apartment above the restaurant that Steven's father and his Uncle Frank own. Their restaurant, The Salmon Nook, is on the main road that leads into Tofino.

Steven's dad is the cook at The Salmon Nook. His specialties are fresh steamed crab, broiled salmon steaks, and seafood chowder. Tourists come from all over to taste his delicious dishes. Most of the seafood for the restaurant is supplied by Uncle Frank and his crew who fish off the coast. When Steven is not in school, he often helps with the restaurant. Sometimes he delivers flyers advertising the specials of the restaurant. The job he likes best is looking for crabs on the beach and bringing them back to his dad. Greg goes to school for most of the year, but from May to September he takes groups of tourists on whale-watching tours.

Activities

Steven enjoys playing with his friends on the beach, collecting driftwood, looking for trails in the forest, kayaking, and canoeing. Most of all, Steven looks forward to the summer when his brother invites him to go out on whale-watching tours. If Steven is lucky, Greg lets him sit beside him as he steers the boat. Steven loves to see the excitement of the tourists when they catch a glimpse of the giant mammals.

The waters around Vancouver Island are popular for whale watching.

19

Living in Campbell River

Name

Sara Assu, age 9

Community

Sara lives in the town of **Campbell River**. The town is a popular place for tourists to go salmon fishing. Laws limit the number of fish that people can catch. These laws make sure that enough salmon are left to naturally replace those caught. The area around Campbell River offers many other opportunities for outdoor activities. Visitors to nearby **Strathcona Provincial Park** often use the town as a base. Today many hotels, shopping centres, and restaurants provide for the needs of 17 000 residents and the many tourists who come to explore the area.

Campbell River is often called "The Salmon Capital of the World."

In Strathcona Provincial Park people can camp, hike, cross-country ski, and downhill ski.

Family

Sara lives with her parents, John and Margaret, and her two younger brothers, Benjamin and James. They live in a three-bedroom house on one of the reserves in the area. Sara likes being able to see the sea from her house.

Sara's dad is a lawyer at the Campbell River Band Office, which is a few kilometres away from the reserve. Her mom is busy at home with Benjamin and James, who do not go to school yet.

Activities

Sara plays on a soccer team and enjoys playing basketball with her friends. She and her friends also have a lot of fun threading beads onto fish lines to make jewellery.

In the summer Sara likes to play on the beach, gather oysters and clams for her family to eat, and fish for salmon. Her Uncle Jimmy works on a fishing boat and has taught her a lot about fishing.

A potlatch is a ceremony held by Northwest Coast Native peoples that includes feasting, dancing, singing, and storytelling.

In the winter Sara enjoys preparing for the potlatch in December. At this important ceremony, everyone in Sara's community celebrates special events in their lives. People often wear ceremonial blankets called button blankets at the potlatch. On these blankets, people sew or attach items that symbolize who they are. Sara is proud when she wears her button blanket to the potlatch. It has her crest, the Salmon Fish, sewn on the back. To prepare for the potlatch, Sara takes singing and dancing lessons at the Thunderbird Hall. Singing songs in Kwakiutl helps Sara learn the language of her people.

Started in 1985, the Totem Poles Project in Duncan represents an ancient art form and features the work of local Native carvers.

Living in Duncan

Name

Krista Harris, age 9

Community

Krista lives near **Duncan**, the business centre of the Cowichan Valley. Duncan is often called the "City of Totems" because there are over 40 totem poles that line its streets. The area near Duncan is the home of the British Columbia Forest Museum Park, which highlights the history of the British Columbia logging industry. Although some people in Duncan still work in traditional farming or logging jobs, more and more people now work in jobs that provide services or goods to the surrounding communities.

Family

Krista lives with her parents, Anne and Bob, her sister, Kari, and her grandparents, Sam and Mary. They live in a farmhouse just outside of the town of Duncan. Her grandparents used to run the farm, but now they rent the fields to a local farmer.

Krista's dad is an engineer. He works for a pulp and paper company. Her mother works for the same company as a forest management researcher. She believes it is important to plan for the future of forests, so that trees are not cut down faster than they can be replaced.

Forestry provides jobs for many people living in or near Duncan.

Activities

Krista enjoys riding her bike and climbing trees. When her family has out-of-town visitors, the family usually takes them to the British Columbia Forest Museum Park. The visit includes taking a ride on the old steam train through the forest. Krista also enjoys showing visitors the totem poles in Duncan and explaining that many of them were hand carved by members of the local Cowichan band.

Tourists enjoy rides on a steam engine train through the British Columbia Forest Museum Park.

In this activity you are going to write a story that tells how people in your community live.

1. Discuss the stories about Steven, Sara, and Krista with a partner:
   - What natural resources can be found in or near each community?
   - How do these resources affect the way people live?
   - If each person moved to another part of the island, what in the person's life might change? What might stay the same?

2. Write a story about life in your community. Think about these questions:
   - Where is your community located?
   - What does the surrounding area look like?
   - What natural resources or physical features are there?
   - In what ways do people in your community use their surroundings?
   - What kinds of jobs and fun activities do you and your family like to do in your community?
   - What is your favourite time of year in your community? Why?

3. Use family photos or pictures of your community to illustrate important points in your story.

With your classmates, put your stories together to make a book about your community.

Discover P.E.I.

What attracts 700 000 visitors every year to an island on Canada's east coast? Prince Edward Island may be Canada's smallest province, but with rich farmland, sandy beaches, and many fishing harbours, it offers people living or visiting there many things to see and do.

Camille and her family have just returned from a trip to Prince Edward Island. During her three-day visit Camille recorded her many discoveries of Prince Edward Island in a travel log.

Our Trip to P.E.I.

Monday, July 7

6:45 A.M.

We got up early to catch the ferry from <u>Cape Tormentine, New Brunswick</u> to Prince Edward Island. There is a long line but the ferry holds 150 cars. Tyrone and I counted the cars in front of us and we're sure we'll get on the next boat.

8:30 A.M.

We landed at <u>Borden</u> and drove north to <u>Summerside</u>. Along the way we saw many farms with fields of potatoes. On some farms we saw dairy cows grazing on grass. Mom asked why the ground is so red. My book on P.E.I. says it's because of the iron in the soil. I'm bringing some back in a jar to show my friends.

9:30 A.M.

We ate breakfast near the harbour in Summerside and watched the boats sail by. Tyrone was so busy drawing on his napkin that he didn't finish his breakfast.

10:45 A.M.

From Summerside we drove west along the southern coast on a highway called <u>Lady Slipper Scenic Drive</u>. We stopped once to take a look at the flowers. We saw mostly lupins and devil's paint brush, but couldn't find a lady's slipper. By July the blooms are dead. The lady's slipper is P.E.I.'s provincial flower. Mom says that, like prairie lilies in Saskatchewan and trilliums in Ontario, lady's slippers are protected by law so that they won't become extinct.

11:30 A.M.

At _Mount Pleasant_ we turned left onto _Highway 2_, the road that runs right through the centre of the island. Just north of Mount Pleasant we saw a small airplane landing at an airfield. At _Carleton_, Lady Slipper Scenic Drive turns left to go along the shore again. It goes along the west coast of the island, but we had to take the main highway to get to the Potato Museum in _O'Leary_.

12:45 P.M.

The museum was interesting. There is so much to know about potatoes! I still can't believe that more than half of the seed potatoes grown in Canada come from P.E.I. After our visit to the museum we returned to Highway 2, and went to _Tignish_ for lunch. We tried the chowder.

4:30 P.M.

From Tignish we turned east toward the coast. We saw fishing boats and people on the wharf cleaning fish. From there, we headed south again along the shore on another part of Lady Slipper Scenic Drive. We went over a large bridge, through _Alberton_, and over two more bridges before getting back to Highway 2 between Carleton and _Portage_. From Portage, we went to _Kensington_ on Highway 2 where we checked in at the Victoria Inn.

I tried lobster for the first time. It was pretty good.
After dinner we went for a drive along the east edge of
<u>Malpeque Bay</u>, through <u>Sea View</u>, and over to
<u>New London</u>. Mom said if we had one extra day we
could have gone tuna fishing here. Maybe next time!
We're back at the Inn and it's almost time for bed, but
not before I read more about Anne of Green Gables.

Tuesday, July 8

10:30 A.M.

This morning we drove to
<u>Cavendish</u> to see Green
Gables House, the setting of
Lucy Maud Montgomery's
stories about Anne. It was
great to see the house I've
been reading about. Now
we're going for a swim at
Cavendish Beach. I've always
wanted to swim in the ocean.

1:00 P.M.

From the beach we went
south again to get back on
Highway 2 at <u>Hunter River</u>.
Now we are in <u>Charlottetown</u>, the capital of P.E.I.
We are going into the Confederation Centre of the Arts
to see a live performance of "Anne of Green Gables."

6:00 P.M.

As we left Charlottetown, I spotted some blue herons in the <u>Hillsborough River</u>. We followed Highway 2 again all the way from Charlottetown to where the highway

ends at <u>Souris</u>. Along the route, at <u>Morell</u>, we left the highway for a short stop at <u>St. Peters Bay</u>—more fishing boats and lobster traps. We are now at the Lighthouse & Beach Motel in Souris.

Wednesday, July 9

9:30 A.M.

We had to get up early to drive to the ferry. We followed Highway 2 back to <u>Dingwells Mills</u> and turned south to get to <u>Montague</u>, where we had breakfast.

10:50 A.M.

Tyrone and I asked if we could take the coast road and stop along the way for a swim. Mom said we had to take the main road from Montague to <u>Wood Islands</u> to catch the next ferry. Along the way we saw more cattle. Mom said some were dairy cows, and others were being raised for beef. We may as well have gone for a swim because the ferry couldn't hold all of the cars lined up. Now we have to wait 50 minutes until the next one leaves for <u>Caribou, Nova Scotia</u>.

To Do

In this activity you are going to work with a group to make a large pictomap of Prince Edward Island.

1. Ask your teacher for an overhead transparency map of P.E.I. Shine the map onto a large piece of mural paper and trace everything that is on it.

2. On the map, show
   - the route that Camille and her family travelled
   - the natural resources and physical features of the island
   - what people do on different parts of the island
   Use information from Camille's log to help you.

3. Discuss your finished pictomap with your classmates:
   - How is life different from place to place on the island? How is it the same?
   - How is life on P.E.I. different from life in your community? How is it the same?

Display your pictomaps in the classroom.

How To

Make a Pictomap

A pictomap is a map that shows information about a place through pictures.

- On your pictomap of P.E.I., label
  - water bodies
  - towns and cities
  - transportation routes

- Use pictures to show
  - types of transportation
  - physical features and natural resources
  - tourist attractions
  - activities of people

- Draw pictures or cut photos from old magazines, maps, or brochures to illustrate your map.

- Think about where to put each picture on the map. Paste or tape each picture near the location of the feature that the picture illustrates.

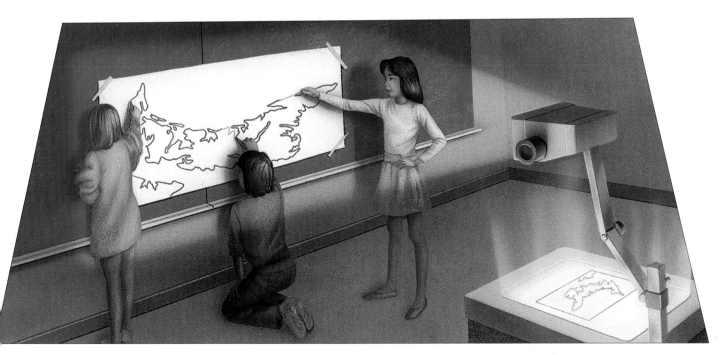

BAFFIN .... BRRR!

Imagine what it would be like
to live on an Arctic island.
What type of weather
would you expect?
How would you travel?
What would you eat?
What would you do in
your spare time?

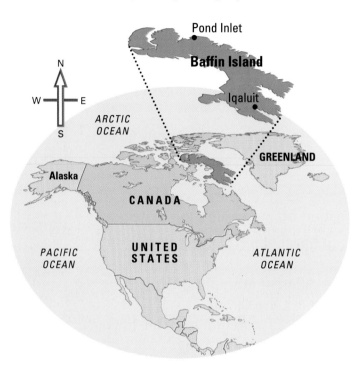

Baffin Island, located in the Arctic region, is the largest
island in Canada. For most of the year, snow and ice
cover this rocky, treeless island, and the surrounding
ocean stays frozen. This is because the average winter
temperature is at least 30 degrees below zero Celsius.
Even in the summer, the temperature is usually only
five or 10 degrees above zero. Despite these difficult
conditions, people have found ways to live on this island
for thousands of years. Read the article "It's Cold Here,
but It's Fun!" to get an idea of what life is like for the
Inuit people who live on Baffin Island today. How are
their lives the same as or different from yours?

It's Cold Here, but It's Fun!

Excerpted from an Owl magazine article,
"It's Cold Here, but It's Fun!"
by Penny Williams

Why is spring such a big deal on Baffin Island? On the shortest winter days in Iqaluit, the sun is only up for three hours. In Pond Inlet, there's no sun for two months!

Brrrrrr? S-s-s-s-Spring's Here!

All the kids nod when Jason, age 12, says, "Spring is when it's really sunny." Winters on Baffin Island are really dark because this part of Earth is tilted away from the sun in winter. In the summer, it's the opposite. So when the sun comes back—even though there's lots of snow and freezing temperatures—it's spring! Mike, 11, shakes his head when the kids talk about how "warm" it is. "We just moved here from southern Ontario and it doesn't feel very warm to me! But it is nice and bright."

Here's How to Eat Out Baffin-Style

Like most other kids, kids on Baffin love to eat burgers and fries. But Inuit (the native Arctic people) also eat fish, birds, and other animals that they catch themselves. By the time they're in grade 6, many kids have shot their first caribou. They're proud of this because it means they're good hunters and helping to provide food for their families and friends. Linda, 13, says, "My family's going to hunt caribou and seals and Arctic char. I hope I shoot a seal this year!" Sharing is important, too. Willie, 12, says, "I just brought part of my first caribou to class. We're going to cook up an 'uju' (stew) with it."

Keep an Eye Out for the Polar Bears!

Kids in most places look for the first robin in spring. But on Baffin, kids look for the first snow bunting. Pond Inlet kids who go out by the open water in spring see whales, walruses, and polar bears. Polar bears can be anywhere, even in their village, so kids always watch out for them. If they see one, they walk away and tell an adult. If it's too close to do that, kids have to curl up in a ball and act dead.

Computers, Kamiks, and Baseball Caps

If you ever meet kids from Baffin Island, don't ask them what it's like to live in an igloo. They may not roll their eyes at you, but you'll get the idea. Pull-eeze! They live in modern houses, watch TV, play computer games, wear baseball caps, and go to a school like you do. But they still do a lot of old things, too— only they do them in a modern way. For instance, people here wear modern clothing but everybody has at least a traditional parka and a favourite pair of kamiks, or sealskin boots. In school kids use computers that work in Inuktitut, the Inuit language, and English.

Hanging Out on an Iceberg

An iceberg is made of old snow—about 2000 years old! Over time, as snow falls on land without melting, it turns into ice, becomes a glacier, and moves slowly towards the ocean. There, chunks as tall as a highrise building break off, fall into the water, and become icebergs. As they float south, some icebergs pass near Pond Inlet. Every winter, some of them get stuck here when the ice freezes. Kids play on them in the spring. Ashley, 10, and Erica, 11, explain, "We slide on them or play soccer. Sometimes pieces of ice fall off. If you don't see it coming, that's really scary."

Modern Kids Discover Old Baffin Ways

Each community on Baffin has its own elders—older Inuit people who know more about the old ways than anybody else. When teachers in Pond Inlet plan a class trip out on the ice, they always ask an elder to come along. Pauline Hewak, who taught here last year explains, "The elders know where all the traditional campsites are, they know how to watch for polar bears, and they can tell when the ice is dangerous." Baffin kids have modern lives now, so it's fun when the school gets an elder to teach them string games, old stories, or igloo-building.

CHECK IT OUT

Baffin Island is very close to the North Pole but it isn't the closest island. Check an atlas or a globe to see which island is closest to the North Pole.

Life on Baffin Island has changed over time. In the past, people living on this island relied on each other and the resources around them to meet their needs. Today, Baffin Island is no longer as isolated as it once was. Airplanes, television, satellite dishes, and computers have allowed people living on Baffin Island to get resources and information from all over the world.

Throughout the world technology has changed the way people live. Think about your community. How has technology changed it over time?

In this activity you are going to interview an adult to find out how technology has changed life in your community.

1. Find someone who has lived in your community for the last 50 or more years.

2. Interview the person about how technology has changed the community. Ask questions such as
   - What modern technologies were available when you were a child?
   - What modern technologies were not available when you were a child?
   - In what ways has modern technology made life for children today different from how it was when you were a child?

3. Present your findings in a report, a taped recording, or a chart. Add pictures or photos to make your presentation more interesting.

Share the information from your interview with your classmates.

How To
Conduct an Interview

Keep these tips in mind as you plan and conduct your interview.

- Decide what you would like to find out. Write a list of questions.

- Choose a person who has the information you need. Tell him or her the purpose of your interview.

- Set up a time and a place to meet with this person.

- Bring a notepad to the interview to write down the answers to your questions. Ask for permission if you want to tape-record or videotape the interview.

- Ask your questions clearly and listen carefully when the other person is talking. Ask any new questions that you think of during the interview.

- Enjoy yourself and remember to thank the person you interviewed.

Islands, Islands Everywhere

To really know what islands are like, you have to get to know many of them. Each one is different so the image you have of an island will change every time you visit or study a new one. Some islands are small; others are large. Some islands are covered with trees; others are covered with snow. Some islands are deserted; others are crowded with people and buildings. The list is endless.

Delta islands

Volcanic island

Coral islands

One of the reasons islands are different from each other is that they are formed in different ways.

Some islands are formed by volcanoes on the ocean floor erupting. When a volcano gets large enough to reach the surface of the ocean, an island is formed.

The growth of coral in shallow water can form ocean islands. Coral is made up of the skeletons of tiny animals called coral polyps. When living polyps die, new ones grow on top of the skeletons. In this way, coral can eventually form a low island above the surface of the ocean.

Some islands—called delta islands—form at the mouths of rivers. They do this because fine soil carried by the moving water of a river builds up when the water slows down.

Some islands are formed when the sea level rises and covers all of the land except the tops of mountains.

Another reason islands are different from each other is that they are always changing. Sometimes islands change because of events in nature, such as an earthquake or a flood. Other times islands change because of people's activities, such as building homes or roads.

CHECK IT OUT

A new volcanic island appeared near Japan in 1986. Try to find the name of this young island.

Bookshelf

You might want to read one of these books to find out more about how islands are formed or changed:

Island
by Lionel Bender (Franklin Watts: New York, 1989)

Islands
by Terry Jennings (Oxford University Press: Toronto, 1988)

Mountaintop islands

Islands Around the World

Greenland
Greenland is the largest island in the world. Most of it is covered with snow and ice. Through the seasons each year the shape of the island changes as the ice melts and freezes again. Check your atlas to find other islands that are covered with snow and ice.

Surtsey
In 1963 an erupting volcano formed a new island called Surtsey near the coast of Iceland. By 1967 the island was almost two kilometres long. The Hawaiian Islands were also formed by volcanoes. In which ocean are the Hawaiian Islands located? How many islands make up this group?

NORTH AMERICA

EUROP

AFRIC

Shemya
Until recently, the small rocky island of Shemya was uninhabited. Now this remote island off the coast of Alaska is a refuelling station for planes flying from Seattle to eastern Asia. Why do you suppose the island is well suited for this purpose?

Trinidad
Continental islands lie close to the mainland because at one time they were joined to it. Some are formed when the sea level changes. Others are formed when a piece of land breaks away from the mainland. Trinidad, located just off the coast of Venezuela, is a continental island. Find one other island that may be a continental island.

PACIFIC OCEAN

Galápagos Islands
The Galápagos Islands, off the coast of Ecuador, are famous for the unusual animals that live there. Scientists think that when a species arrives on an island, it can change over the years into a new species that exists nowhere else in the world. Find the name of one of these unique animals.

SOUTH AMERICA

ATLANTIC OCEAN

One centimetre on this map is the same as 1100 kilometres on the ground.

0	1100	2200	3300

kilometres

N
W — E
S

To Do

In this activity you will find out how some islands in the world were formed or changed.

1. Read the descriptions for the islands identified on the world map.

2. With a partner, answer the question or complete the activities following each description.

3. Record your responses.

Compare your responses with another pair of classmates.

ASIA

PACIFIC OCEAN

INDIAN OCEAN

AUSTRALIA

ANTARCTICA

Kansai International Airport
In 1994, Kansai International Airport opened on a small, artificial island off the east coast of Honshū Island in Japan. This is the first time an island has ever been created for something as large as an international airport. Why do you think the airport was not built on the main island?

Kwajalein
The largest atoll in the world is Kwajalein in the Marshall Islands of the Pacific Ocean. An atoll is a circle- or horseshoe-shaped coral island with a lagoon in the middle. Check resources at home, in the classroom, or in the library to find out how an atoll is formed.

Mauritius
A lot of the forests on the island of Mauritius have been cleared for farmland. Much of the remaining forest has been made into nature reserves. Why might the government protect the forests in this way?

LIFE IN A CROWDED PLACE

When a lot of people live on an island, there are not always enough resources to meet everyone's needs. Often people living on crowded islands have to find creative ways to meet their needs.

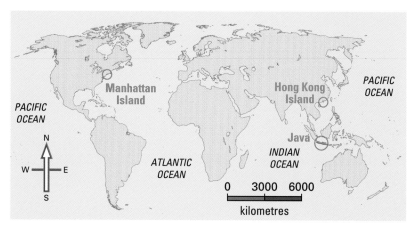

Hong Kong Island, Manhattan Island, and Java are all islands with very large populations. These islands weren't always so crowded. Many years ago, small groups of people arrived on these islands and decided to develop small villages. Over time more and more people arrived and the population on each island grew. Today, Manhattan Island, Hong Kong Island, and Java are among the most heavily populated places in the world.

With a partner, read about how people on these islands have adapted to life in a crowded place. Discuss these questions:

• What problems has crowding caused?
• How have people tried to solve the problems?
• What new problems have people created?
• How have the solutions affected the plants, animals, and people on the island?

Hong Kong Island

Hong Kong Island is a tiny island near the southern coast of China. Over 1.3 million people live on this small island.

Since most of this island is hilly or mountainous, there is very little flat space for people to build homes. To create more flat land, people have added to the north shore of the island. To do this, they have built barriers in the sea, pumped out the water, and filled in the space with rock and soil.

To get the most use out of the small amount of land on Hong Kong Island, many highrise buildings have been built. Most of the people on the island live in small apartments in these buildings.

Other people live in the harbour on houseboats or fishing boats. These floating communities include grocery stores, schools, and homes—so people don't even have to set foot on land!

Manhattan Island

New York, the largest city in the United States, is located both on the mainland and several surrounding islands. A large part of the city is located on Manhattan Island. This tiny island has a population of 1.5 million people.

Since most people on Manhattan Island live and work in highrise buildings, planners try to leave space for rest and relaxation. The largest park, Central Park, contains a zoo, some lakes, an open-air concert area, and lots of trees and grassy fields.

On Manhattan Island, people need to be creative to find space for recreation, relaxation, and exercise. Some people even use the rooftops of the buildings.

Getting around in a large city like New York can be very difficult. If everyone drove a car, there would be so many cars that no one could get anywhere. The city has planned many ways to help move people around. For example, people can take subways, ferries, trains, and taxi cabs.

Java

Java is in the group of islands that make up the nation of Indonesia. It is the most populated island in the world, with 112 million people.

To increase the area where food can be grown, farmers on Java have built huge, flat terraces.

The population of Java is increasing at the rate of two million people per year. One way the government handles the population increase is to build roads to more remote areas of Java. This encourages people to move from the cities and the lowland areas to the island's less-populated hilly areas.

Another way the government handles the population increase is to encourage people to move to the less-populated surrounding islands.

To Do

In this activity you are going to identify problems and think of solutions for people living on a crowded island.

1. Examine the map and read the information about an imaginary island—Marcus Island.

2. Identify two problems that might occur as a result of too many people living on the island. Think about
   - What are the features of this island?
   - Where do people live on this island?
   - How might the island's features create a problem?

3. Think of a solution for each problem you have identified. Think about
   - How could the solutions for crowding on Hong Kong Island, Manhattan Island, or Java help the people of Marcus Island?
   - How could the features of Marcus Island help solve each problem?
   - What possible effect might your ideas have on the natural environment or on the people?

4. Draw an illustration and write a description for each of your solutions.

Share your solutions with your classmates.

FOR YOUR INFORMATION

Usually the word "island" describes a piece of land surrounded by water. However, "island" can also be used to describe anything that is surrounded in some way by something else. Traffic islands, kitchen islands, and display islands in stores are other types of islands.

Marcus Island

Marcus Island is a small mountainous island located near the equator in the Pacific Ocean. It has swamps near its lake and rivers. The first people on the island came from South America and made their way to the island on reed rafts. Later, English and French pirates used the island as a base. The descendants of these groups are a small portion of the people who now live on Marcus Island. Over the past 50 years many people have moved to the island. The island does not attract many tourists because the beaches are small and rocky and much of the land is rough and mountainous.

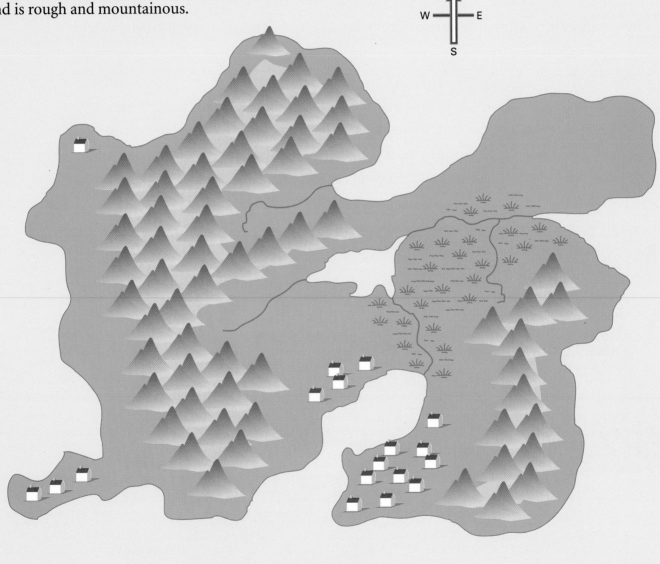

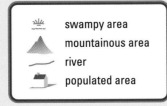

⚘	swampy area
▲	mountainous area
～	river
⌂	populated area

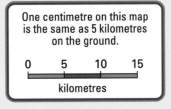

One centimetre on this map is the same as 5 kilometres on the ground.

0   5   10   15

kilometres

Once Upon an Island

Islands all over the world are used as settings for stories. Often an island's location, physical features, natural resources, or people are an important part of the stories. These same things are also part of everyday life on islands throughout the world.

These collector cards give you some information about four islands in the world. Match each of the island collector cards with one of the stories on pages 48 to 51. Write down your choices and then compare them with a classmate.

ALCATRAZ

Average Temperature	**Average Precipitation**
Jan. 10°C	Jan. 11.9 cm
July 15°C	July 0.03 cm

TORTUGA

Average Temperature
Jan. 23.9°C
July 27.8°C

Average Precipitation
Jan. 14.5 cm
July 3.5 cm

WHITE ISLAND

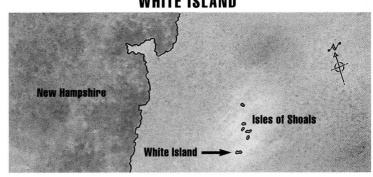

Average Temperature
Jan. -6.7°C
July 21°C

Average Precipitation
Jan. 7.1 cm
July 7.4 cm

SABLE ISLAND

Average Temperature
Jan. -0.2°C
July 15.7°C

Average Precipitation
Jan. 8.5 cm
July 7.4 cm

During the seventeenth century several French adventurers made a living on some of the Caribbean islands by hunting and selling the meat of wild cattle, horses, and swine to passing ships. To prepare the meat, they cut it into thin strips, salted and smoked it, and dried it in the sun. This process was called buccanning, and the adventurers became known as "buccaneers." This letter to a friend back in France describes the adventures of one buccaneer.

Dear François,   May 5, 1654

Since I last wrote, my life has changed a lot. A while ago many of us moved from Hispaniola to a small island nearby shaped like a huge sea turtle. The island's harbour makes it a safe place for passing ships to stop. With more people stopping on the island we are preparing and selling more meat than ever. But more changes are still to come. Let me explain.

Recently some of our countrymen arrived to join us. One of the newcomers, Pierre le Grand, was not happy to spend his days preparing and selling meat. Instead he and a crew of men attacked a passing Spanish galleon and captured its treasures. Now many buccaneers are joining Pierre and capturing rich Spanish ships instead of wild cattle. Life as a pirate can be dangerous but there is the chance to become very rich. I have decided to go with Pierre on his next trip. The next time I write it will be to tell you of my adventures on the high seas.

Your friend,
Louis

ALONE NEAR A CROWD

He came to the island as a visitor—one of the hundreds of tourists who take the short boat ride each day. The trip to the island was not his first; he had once been forced to live on "The Rock" for 12 years. He entered a large building and looked into the small room that had been his cell.

In a space no bigger than the top of a ping-pong table, he had spent many hours lying on a bed reading. During his jail term, over 6000 books from the building's library had helped to fill his long days.

He and the other tourists walked into the dining hall. Through its windows he could see cruise ships sailing by and hear the sounds of a city. The city was only a short distance away but the strong, cold saltwater currents surrounding the small island had always stopped people from leaving "The Rock."

HIDDEN DANGER

From the air it looks like a new moon. In reality, it is a 40 km sandbar that stretches far beneath the surface of the water, waiting to trap ships that come too close.

In 1760, Major Elliott, his wife, and their two children travelled through these waters on their way to New York. Without warning the ship hit the northeast tip of the sandbar and was grounded. A quick-thinking crew member tied a rope around his waist and swam to shore, where he secured it. Elliott and his wife strapped their children to their backs and, along with the rest of the crew, used the rope to make their way through the cold water to land.

There were no people living on the sandbar island, and the only source of fresh food came from the cattle and wild horses that grazed on the grass of the sand dunes. To survive, the crew made several trips to the shipwreck for dried food and building materials. Finally, after two cold months, a passing fishing schooner came to their rescue.

Celia Thaxter was a poet and writer who spent many years of her childhood living on an island. In these excerpts from her journal, she writes of her experiences.

FOR **Y**OUR **I**NFORMATION

The oldest lighthouse in North America is located on Sambro Island in the mouth of Halifax Harbour. The lighthouse became fully automated after the last lightkeeper retired in 1988.

September 5, 1839
I will always remember my first sight of the island where we lived after my family and I left the mainland. My father was to be the new lighthouse keeper. How excited I was on that first long sail to our island. We entered the little stone cottage that is now our home. How curious it seems with its low, whitewashed ceiling and deep window seats that show the great thickness of the walls made to keep out the sea. We slept that evening with the sound of water all around us for the first time.

March 3, 1843
We survive many a dreary winter by keeping to our fireside and living with the plants, singing birds, books, and playthings that Mother and Father were wise enough to bring from the mainland. In the stormy winter, no supply boats venture out to us. Father holds school at the kitchen table. He is teaching us reading and arithmetic. Most of all, I like to listen to Father recite poetry written by famous people.

May 16, 1843
Now it is spring, and our neighbours from Star Island rowed across. It is a pity they have no children for us to play with, but it was good to see someone else beside the family. The pilot boat from Portsmouth also arrived and brought us letters and newspapers that told us the news of the past months.

October 17, 1845
The weather has turned much cooler, but, bundled up, we still go out to the beach to play. Today my brother and I dragged up long seaweed from the water. Mussels were fastened to its roots. We carried those home to be cooked by Mother. Fried in crumbs or batter, they were as good as oysters.

December 5, 1846
This morning I have crept out of the still house before anyone was awake. I look to the sea lying still like a mirror, the water drawn away from the rich brown rocks. I would see a sail or two and not hear a sound. When I see those things, I know my island home is very special indeed.

To Do

In this activity you are going to make a collector card for an island and write a story that tells something about life on that island.

1. Gather information about a real island or describe an imaginary one.

2. Make a collector card. On the front of the card draw a picture of the island. On the back of the card include
   - the name of the island
   - a map of the island showing its location
   - the island's average temperature and precipitation

3. Write a story about something that actually happened or could happen on the island. Include clues about
   - the island's location
   - the island's physical features
   - the island's natural resources
   - where and how the inhabitants of the island live or lived

Match the collector cards and stories created by your classmates.

Tech Tools

You may wish to use a desktop publishing program to design your island collector card and write your story.

BUILD AN ISLAND

These pictures show some of the islands people live on. If you could live on any type of island in the world, what would you choose?

To Do

In this activity you are going to work in a group to build a model of an inhabited island.

1. Discuss what features your island will have. Your island should be no larger than one kilometre by one kilometre in real life. Choose one group member to record all of the ideas on a list.

2. Draw a map of the island. Show where each item on the list will be located.

3. Decide on the materials you will need to build the island. Think about what materials will best represent the different features of the island.

4. Discuss and decide what each member of the group will do to help build the model.

5. As you build the model, keep the map nearby to remind you of how you want the island to look.

6. Try to represent the size of each item on the model as accurately as possible.

7. Once your model is complete, organize a tour for visitors to the island. Include information about
   - important features of the island
   - what people can see and do
   - future changes to the island

Go on a tour of the islands created by your classmates.

For Your Information

If you look at a globe or a map of the world you will notice that islands often occur in groups or long chains. These are called archipelagos. The largest archipelago in the world is the country of Indonesia with over 13 000 islands.

How To

Plan an Island Model

Think about these questions as you plan your island model.

- Where in the world will the island be located?

- What natural features will your island have? Will it have beaches? mountains? streams? forests?

- What natural resources will the island have? Will it have water? food? forests?

- How many people will live on the island?

- What features made by people will the island have? Will it have buildings? roads? bridges?

- How will people on the island get food, water, and electricity?

- How will people get to and around the island?

- What will people do on the island?

- What things that people need will be made using the resources on the island? What things will be transported to the island?

How To

Represent Size

Use these guidelines to help you represent the size of each item on your island as accurately as possible:

- Look over the list of items for your model island.

- Put all of the items in order from largest to smallest. For example: mountains are largest, houses are smaller than mountains, and people are smaller than houses.

- Use this list to help you build the model.

People who make models often use a scale to correctly represent each object in a reduced size. If your group would like to build your model "to scale" ask your teacher or a parent for help.

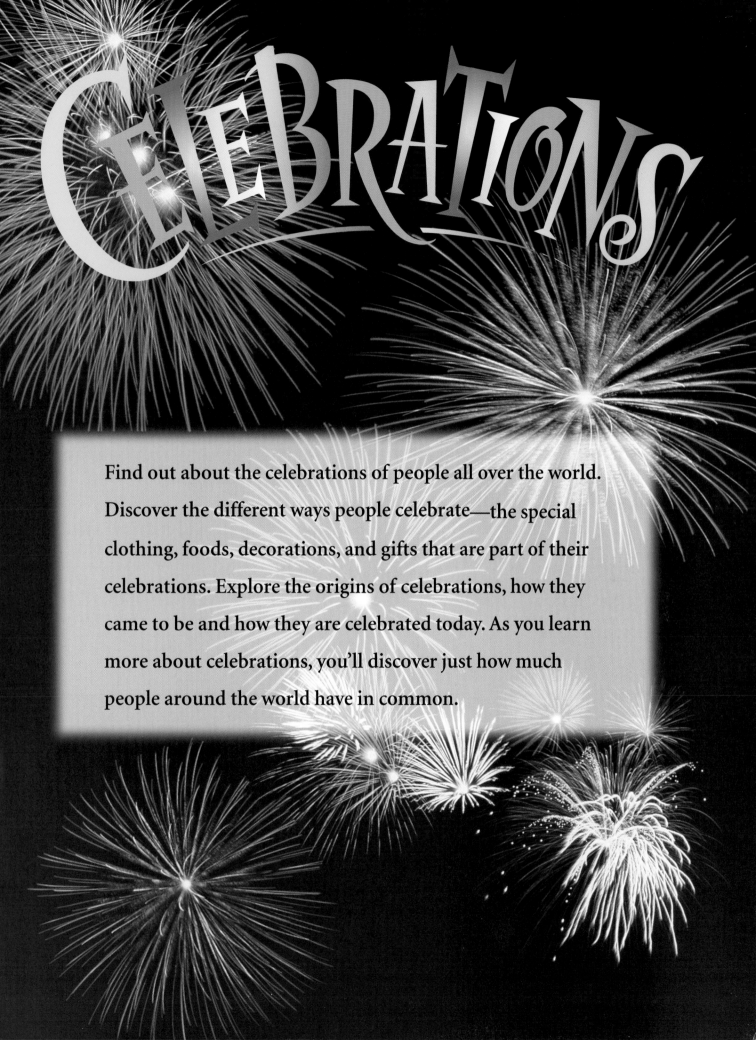

CELEBRATIONS

Find out about the celebrations of people all over the world.
Discover the different ways people celebrate—the special
clothing, foods, decorations, and gifts that are part of their
celebrations. Explore the origins of celebrations, how they
came to be and how they are celebrated today. As you learn
more about celebrations, you'll discover just how much
people around the world have in common.

Celebrate What? Celebrate When?

As we live our lives day after day, through 365 days every year, we set apart some days as different from others. These are special times of celebration. Take some time to learn about those special days— the exciting and joyous celebrations of our lives.

Celebrations Through the Ages

Adapted from Let's Celebrate! *by Caroline Parry*

What is your favourite day of the year? Chances are it's your birthday. And chances are you celebrate when that special day comes around! But don't stop celebrating when your birthday's over.

Kinds of Special Days

In Canada there are more than 250 other special days to celebrate. Many of these are also birthdays, perhaps of a province or a famous person. Others are anniversaries of special events. Still other celebrations are tied to the seasons. For instance, many people hold festivals in the springtime, to celebrate changes like plants beginning to grow and young animals being born.

Celebrations Long Ago

Many of the festivals and special days we celebrate are hundreds or even thousands of years old. Because of this, they have their roots in a time that we can hardly even imagine. Although you may have grown up in a time of supermarkets and fast foods, there was a time, many years ago, where the most important part of all people's lives was survival. Every day was a struggle to stay alive. Getting enough food to eat was a problem to be faced every day. People believed that ceremonies and festivals would bring them good crops or good hunting or fishing. For example, they might hold a ceremony to shorten the winter storms and bring on spring. They held ceremonies to help make changes happen.

Long ago, our ancestors knew that the sun helped things grow, so many early ceremonies were held to strengthen the sun. The sun's strongest and weakest periods—as well as the mid-points of its cycle—were key times for ceremonies. Fire usually symbolizes the sun. Can you think of celebrations today that include fire ceremonies? How do you use fire in your everyday celebrations at home?

People role-playing an ancient sun festival of the Inca people in Peru, South America

Men of the Kalahari in Botswana, Africa dance the ostrich dance. This dance celebrates rainwater. In everyday life, ostrich eggs are used to carry water.

Our ancestors long ago also knew that, along with the life-giving rays of the sun, water helped things grow. That is why rain prayers—either to make rain fall, or in thanks for rain—and other water customs were a big part of early festivals.

These seasonal festivals were the very first celebrations. Since then, people have added new kinds of celebrations to their lives, like religious celebrations (to worship their god) and patriotic or cultural celebrations (to honour their country and the traditions of the people who came from that country). In Canada we're especially lucky. From the beginning of time, different groups of Native peoples have developed a rich variety of festivals. Then, as explorers, immigrant workers, and refugees came to settle in Canada, they brought with them the special customs and holidays of their home countries. Little by little the kinds of celebrations happening in this country began to grow. Recent immigrants to Canada from all parts of the world have added their holidays. As people bring their many rich traditions to this country, Canada becomes a more interesting place to live.

Bookshelf

Two books that can give you lots of information about the special occasions celebrated by Canadians are

Let's Celebrate!
by Caroline Parry (Kids Can Press: Toronto, 1987)

Canada Celebrates Multiculturalism
by Bobbie Kalman (Crabtree: Niagara-on-the-Lake, 1993)

FOR YOUR INFORMATION

Most holidays are celebrated once a year. Some of them are held on the same date on the calendar every year. Others are held on different dates on the calendar every year. This chart gives some examples.

HOLIDAY	DATE	REASON
Canada Day	July 1	The date does not change because it is an important date in history.
Remembrance Day	November 11	
Victoria Day	Monday before May 24	The date changes so that people can enjoy a long weekend.
Thanksgiving	Second Monday in October	
Easter	The weekend after the first full moon after the first day of spring	The date changes because of old traditions involving the moon and the seasons.

CHECK IT OUT

What other Canadian national holidays are celebrated on the same date every year? Find another example of a holiday that is celebrated on a different date this year as compared to last year.

How Celebrations Change

However, it may not be as easy for immigrants to observe the old festivals here in Canada as it was in the country they left. Often customs are changed for a number of reasons. For one thing, the Canadian climate affects holidays. For example, a festival that's held outdoors in India may take place in the middle of the Canadian winter, so the celebration must be changed to take place indoors. The Canadian work week can also interfere with some holidays. Often, holidays are moved to the closest weekend. Holidays can change because people sometimes lose their sense of community and pride in their heritage when they leave their old homes.

Although some celebrations may be dropped, others have grown in new ways in the New World or have been proudly remembered and revived. Often new situations in Canada have led to new festivities. Perhaps people in your own community are involved in a new festivity. Think about it!

To Do

In this activity you are going to make a chart of all the celebrations you know.

1. List the celebrations you know.

2. Compare your lists with the lists of two or three other students.

3. Figure out in which season each celebration occurs. Then write the celebrations onto the form "Celebrations All Year Long."

4. Discuss ways of grouping celebrations together. For example,
   – "Celebrations with Presents"
   – "Celebrations with Special Foods"

5. Show your celebrations grouped together in new ways on a chart.

Put your charts up around the classroom for everyone to see.

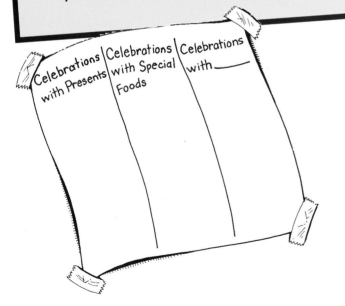

How To

Discuss in a Group

Use these points when you discuss in a group.

- Choose a spokesperson.

- Choose a recorder.

- Let the spokesperson present the topic.

- Let everyone think about the topic.

- Let each person give one idea about the topic.

- Listen when others are talking.

- Raise your hand when you want to say something.

- Let the recorder write down the ideas.

- Read over what the recorder wrote and add any ideas the recorder missed.

Celebrations Near and Far

Picture in your mind a beautiful flower garden. You can see how each flower has its own colour and its own shape. What you do not see is how each flower has its own roots, giving it life, feeding it, and holding it in the earth.

Canadian people and their celebrations are like flowers with lots of different colours and shapes. Like flowers, people have roots that hold them up and make them feel strong because they belong to a group. You share your roots with your family and others. The roots and customs of all Canadians make Canada a colourful and interesting place.

The first Canadians were the Native peoples. They had many celebrations and customs before settlers from other lands ever came to Canada.

Thousands of years later, English and French explorers arrived looking for new lands and new routes to other places. Many English and French people settled in Canada. They told wonderful stories about this land to encourage others to move here, and before long many people did.

Today, Canada is made up of people from Africa; North, Central, and South America; Asia; Europe; Australia; and the Caribbean islands. These places include several countries and groups of people. As members of these groups make Canada their new home, Canada has grown to be a country with many groups or cultures— a "multicultural" country.

People have been moving to Canada for hundreds of years. Members of your family may have first come to this country as long ago as the 1600s. If your ancestors were settlers, they came from somewhere, and they brought customs and traditions with them. If you are a member of a native group, then your ancestors have always been in this country with their own language and customs.

The Sun Dance has been celebrated by Plains people such as the Blackfoot for hundreds of years. The Sun Dance medicine lodge (at the back of the picture) was built on the fifth day of the celebration. Weather dancers outside the lodge would dance for sunny weather.

63

Moving to a New Place

When people leave their country for a new home, they take things with them to remind them of their roots. Some of the things are objects you can touch and see, like photographs. They also take things you cannot touch or hold, like their language and their traditions. What things would you take with you if you moved to a new place? How would these items remind you of your roots? Try to think about at least one item that cannot be seen or touched (perhaps a song, a story, or a celebration).

You might be surprised at how many of Canada's celebrations were brought here by people arriving from other countries. The photograph on this page and pages 65 and 66 show some celebrations. Try to guess the place where each celebration started. Your choices are

- Caribbean Islands
- China
- Ukraine
- Germany
- Iceland
- Scotland
- United States

The answers are on pages 68, 69, and 70.

1

Islendingadagurinn is enjoyed by many Canadians in Manitoba. Guess which country's people started this celebration.

2

Thanksgiving and its customs came from another country. Which country do you think it is?

Caribana is a big summer event in Ontario. Which part of the world do you think gave this celebration to Canada?

3

4

The Highland Games are held in many places in Canada. Choose the country you think these games came from.

5

In the month of October, many Canadians attend Oktoberfest. What place do you think first celebrated this festival?

6

Vesna is a popular celebration every spring in Saskatchewan. Where do you think it started?

7

Sun Nin takes place every year in many places in Canada. Where do you think it came from?

To Do

In this activity you are going to find out about one of your family's celebrations.

1. Choose a celebration that is important to your family.

2. Find out
   – when the celebration is
   – why the celebration is important
   – what happens at the celebration
   – what other countries have the celebration
   – anything else that you think is interesting about the celebration

3. Choose two or three interesting facts about the celebration and write them down in point form on a sheet of paper.

4. Draw a picture about the celebration on a sheet of paper.

Share your celebration sheets with each other.

How To

Find Facts About a Topic

Here are some ways to get information about a topic like a celebration:

• Ask someone in your family.

• Ask someone in your community.

• Look up the name of the topic in an encyclopedia book or a CD-ROM encyclopedia.

• Look up the name of the topic in a subject catalogue at the library. The catalogue lists books about the topic that you can find on the shelves. Look in the books for facts.

Highland Games

Fact 1

Fact 2

Fact 3

CELEBRATIONS FROM CANADA'S NEIGHBOURHOOD

1 **ISLENDINGADAGURINN: Iceland**

In 1890, a group of Icelandic immigrant families had a picnic in Manitoba to remember Iceland, their first home. This annual get-together has become a weekend celebration called "Islendingadagurinn," with sports competitions, dances, concerts, and other events. It is open to all Canadians and tourists who want to share in the pride and joy of Icelandic Canadians.

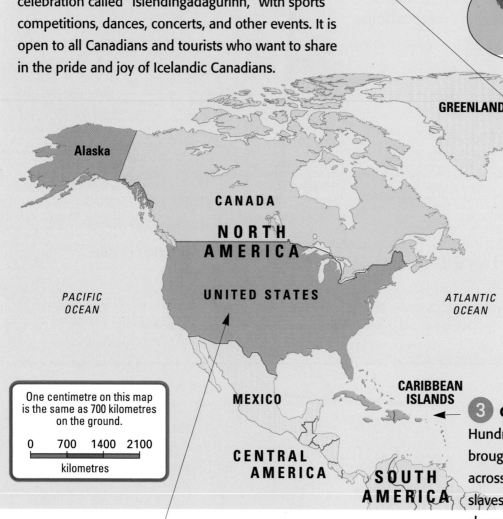

One centimetre on this map is the same as 700 kilometres on the ground.

0   700   1400   2100
kilometres

2 **THANKSGIVING: United States**

Thanksgiving was first celebrated by Pilgrim settlers and Native peoples in the United States. Our Canadian Thanksgiving has borrowed many traditions from the American celebration, like eating turkey, cranberries, squash, and pumpkin.

3 **CARIBANA: Caribbean Islands**

Hundreds of years ago, traders brought people from West Africa across the Atlantic Ocean to work as slaves. In the Caribbean Islands, slavery went on for 200 years. It ended in 1834. To celebrate, people on the island of Trinidad started a festival. The Caribana festival in Canada was created from the traditions of this celebration. It is held every summer with special food, music, dance, and a spectacular parade.

CELEBRATIONS FROM ACROSS THE ATLANTIC OCEAN

4 HIGHLAND GAMES: Scotland

Hundreds of years ago, families (called "clans") got together in Scotland and held sports competitions to improve their hunting and battle skills. These competitions were later called the "Highland Games." Scottish immigrants have brought this tradition with them as they have moved to new homes all over the world. Some of the events include races, pole vault, throwing a heavy pole called a "caber," Highland dancing, and bagpipe playing.

One centimetre on this map is the same as 200 kilometres on the ground.

0   200   400   600
kilometres

ATLANTIC OCEAN

FINLAND

SWEDEN

NORWAY

N

W   E

S

RUSSIA

NORTHERN IRELAND

SCOTLAND

ESTONIA

LATVIA

DENMARK

IRELAND

GREAT BRITAIN

THE NETHERLANDS

RUSSIA

LITHUANIA

BELARUS

WALES

ENGLAND

EUROPE

POLAND

GERMANY

BELGIUM

LUXEMBOURG

CZECH REPUBLIC

FRANCE

SLOVAKIA

LIECHTENSTEIN

SWITZERLAND

AUSTRIA

HUNGARY

ROMANIA

5 OKTOBERFEST: Germany

Farmers in Germany celebrate the time of harvest. In October, they harvest the flowers from a vine called the "hop" vine to make drinks. In the early 1800s, the hop harvest fair in Germany was combined with horse races celebrating the marriage of a German prince. This event grew into a two-week-long festival. In the 1960s, the Oktoberfest tradition was brought to Canada. It is celebrated as much by non-German Canadians as it is by German immigrants and their families.

CELEBRATIONS FROM FAR AWAY

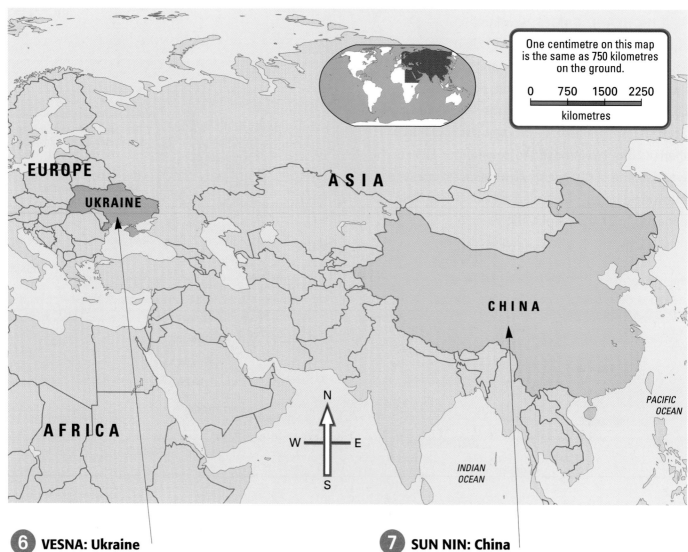

6 VESNA: Ukraine

For hundreds of years, Ukrainians have celebrated the beginning of spring because it brought warm, sunny weather and rain for growing crops. When Ukrainians came to Canada, they kept up their spring celebrations. In 1973, a group of Ukrainian Canadians in Saskatoon started a big spring festival called "Vesna," which is the Ukrainian word for "spring." Vesna has become the world's largest Ukrainian festival, with art and jewellery shows, singing, dancing, and food.

7 SUN NIN: China

"Sun Nin" means "new year" in Chinese. For centuries, people in China have been celebrating their new year after the autumn harvest and before the start of spring. They have also used this time to celebrate everybody's birthday, all at once! Their traditions include spending time with family, remembering ancestors, eating lots of delicious food, giving gifts, and holding a special parade with a Dragon Dance and a Lion Dance. Many Chinese immigrants in Canada have carried on these traditions.

All Dressed Up!

Think about the day the class picture is taken. What do you wear? Why do you think you might spend more time getting your clothes ready than you do on a normal school day?

Some events make us spend more time choosing clothes, getting the clothes ready, and asking others how we look. These events are often times of celebrations. When do you get all dressed up?

Special clothes often hold lots of meaning for people who wear them and for people who see them. Just think about the special clothing you see on people marching in a parade—you can tell different groups apart by the clothes they wear. A very popular parade takes place at the opening ceremonies of the Olympic Games. While all the Olympic team members wear athletic warm-up clothing, each team has chosen its own colours and designs to carry special meaning. Items with special meanings are called symbols.

Try to find out what the Canadian team uniform looked like from the last summer Olympic games. What do you think the colours symbolize? What do you think the design symbolizes?

The opening parade of the 1992 Barcelona Olympic Games. Athletes from Spain are passing by.

CHECK IT OUT

Think of your favourite sports team. It may be a local or national team for any sport. What do their uniforms look like? What reasons can you think of for the uniform's colours and design? What do they symbolize?

Special Clothes for Clubs

Some children belong to clubs or groups that have uniforms. The uniforms they wear show that they are interested in the club's activities. Their uniforms also say that they want to belong to a larger group of people with the same interests and values. Maybe you are part of a group that wears a special hat in a special way, or a special colour, or a special jacket.

Special Clothes for Birthdays

For some people, birthdays are times for dressing up. Read what this boy from Paraguay wears to a birthday party.

The New Suit

by Nidia Sanabria de Romero

Striped suit,
a terrific tie,
buttoned shoes
and brown socks—
my outfit
for the party.

And the recommendations
drove me crazy—
—Don't eat ice cream
because it might drip.
—Juice, drink it slowly
since it dribbles.
—And nothing about
chocolate bombs
that might explode!
Happy birthday!
Who's that stuffed breathless
inside a tight suit?

Next year will be different.
I'll wear old clothes,
be ready to dribble,
and enjoy
ice cream, cake, and everything else.

Dressing-up customs have been passed down to us from our parents, our grandparents, and further back than our grandparents' grandparents. Why do you think these customs stay the same?

CELEBRATION CLOTHING

Years ago, people in different countries had their own styles of dressing up for celebrations. In modern times, many people have moved to different countries with their celebration clothing. This map shows where some kinds of celebration clothing were first created.

CANADA

NORTH AMERICA

Canada

Italy

GUINEA

PACIFIC OCEAN

ATLANTIC OCEAN

SOUTH AMERICA

BOLIVIA

Bolivia

Guinea

AROUND THE WORLD

One centimetre on this map is the same as 1000 kilometres on the ground.

0   1000   2000   3000
kilometres

N
W   E
S

EUROPE

ASIA

ISRAEL

INDIA

JAPAN

Japan

INDIAN OCEAN

PACIFIC OCEAN

PAPUA NEW GUINEA

AFRICA

India

AUSTRALIA

Israel

Papua New Guinea

To Do

In this activity you are going to draw and describe how people around the world dress up for celebrating.

1. In a group, choose a country or group of people whose celebration clothing you will research.

2. Find out what that country's or that group's celebration clothing looks like.
   - Ask someone from that country or group for information.
   - Look in an encyclopedia or a subject catalogue in the library for information.

3. Draw a picture of the clothing on a sheet of paper.

4. Write facts about the celebration on another sheet of paper. Write about
   - the country or group of people that created the clothing
   - the celebrations where people wear the clothing
   - what you think the clothing symbolizes

Put together all the sheets from all the groups to make a class catalogue of celebration clothing.

Country: Bolivia
Celebration:
Symbols:

FEAST-I-VAL

How important is food in our lives? Food is important even if we're not hungry. At a birthday party, after you've had a big meal and are bursting at the seams, you might still have a piece of birthday cake. Eating cake is part of celebrating the special occasion of a birthday.

People from all parts of the world use food to mark special occasions. If one kind of food is always eaten at a celebration, it becomes the traditional food for the celebration. For example, some Canadians always eat turkey on Thanksgiving.

Tech Tools

You can use a computer software program graphing to graph the results of your CHECK IT OUT survey.

Harvest Celebrations

Thanksgiving is a holiday celebrating the harvest, when grains and other foods are ripe and can be collected and stored away before winter comes. Harvest is celebrated by people all over the world. Their celebrations go back to the days when all people grew their own food—the days before there were big cities. Because people were always thankful when they had gathered their crops for the winter, they would celebrate. Naturally, a big part of this celebration was the food itself.

There are still many cultures where people grow all their own food. These people are especially thankful at harvest time. If your family grows vegetables in a garden, you know the great feeling you get when you have a good crop.

The Ojibwa Wild Rice Harvest

The Ojibwa people of North America celebrate the wild rice harvest each year at the end of the summer. Wild rice is a sacred food for the Ojibwa people, who have been gathering it in the Great Lakes region for 2500 years. Since the 1950s, some people have brought wild rice into Saskatchewan and Alberta, where it is now grown as well.

Wild rice is not really rice at all, even though it is cooked like rice and tastes like rice. It is the seed of a thick, long grass that grows in rivers. To harvest the rice, the Ojibwa go by canoe to where it is growing and knock it into the canoe using long sticks.

The Ojibwa follow old customs to prepare the rice for eating. First they heat the rice so that its outer covering, called the "husk," cracks. Then someone stomps on the rice in a bucket so the husk separates from the seed inside. Next the rice from the bucket is tossed into the air so the husks will blow away in the wind. When the leftover seed is cooked, families gather to share the meal. At the meal, an older family member may talk about how good it is to follow the old ways and teach them to the children, so that the Ojibwa harvest customs will stay alive.

Ojibwa people harvest wild rice growing in Leech Lake, Minnesota.

To Do

In this activity you are going to write a menu for one of the world's harvest celebrations.

1. Find out the name of a harvest celebration.
   – Ask family or friends.
   – Look up "harvest" in a library subject catalogue.

2. Find facts about the celebration like
   – which group of people celebrates it
   – where the group lives
   – what foods they eat

3. Show what you learn in a menu.

   a) Write in the menu
   – the foods of the celebration
   – other interesting facts you found

   b) Draw in the menu
   – a picture to show the food or part of the celebration
   – a map to show where in the world the celebration takes place

Share your menus to see which customs are the same in different harvest celebrations around the world.

FOR **Y**OUR **I**NFORMATION

Here is a list of some harvest celebrations:
- The Algonkian Wild Rice Harvest (in Canada)
- The Northern Cree Wild Rice Harvest (in Canada)
- The Iroquois Harvest Ceremony (in Canada and the United States)
- Oktoberfest (in Germany and other parts of the world)
- Onam (in southern India and other parts of the world)
- Sukkot (celebrated by many Jewish people in many parts of the world)

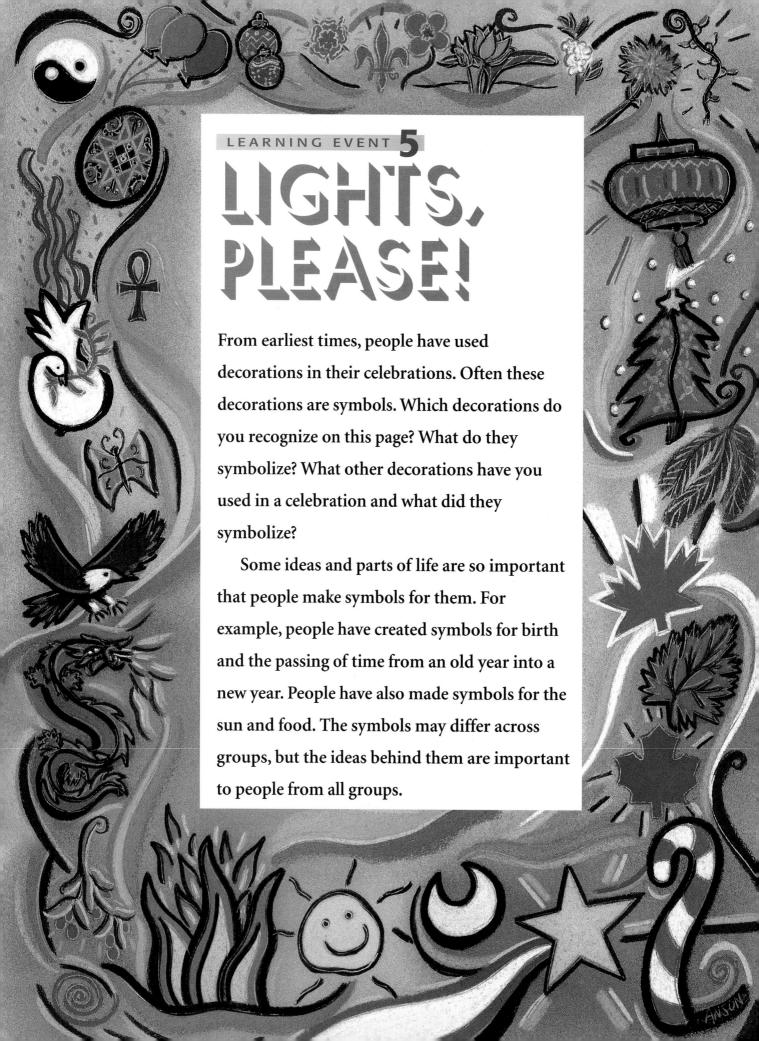

LIGHTS, PLEASE!

From earliest times, people have used decorations in their celebrations. Often these decorations are symbols. Which decorations do you recognize on this page? What do they symbolize? What other decorations have you used in a celebration and what did they symbolize?

Some ideas and parts of life are so important that people make symbols for them. For example, people have created symbols for birth and the passing of time from an old year into a new year. People have also made symbols for the sun and food. The symbols may differ across groups, but the ideas behind them are important to people from all groups.

You may know the saying "There's more to this than meets the eye." Sometimes a detective will use this saying when he or she is trying to solve a crime or mystery. We could use the same words when talking about the decorations used in celebrations.

When we see a decoration, what meets the eye? Many times it's a brightly coloured, beautiful design. Long ago the decoration had a meaning for the people who created it. Sometimes the meaning is simple and obvious. Other times, the meaning has become lost over time, and it's very hard to explain why the decoration looks the way it does. There are even times when a decoration used in a celebration makes us feel something that we can't put into words. We can't say what we feel, but we share the feeling with other members of a group.

During the celebration called "Kwanzaa," many African-Canadians and African-Americans use lit candles as decorations. The light of each candle is a symbol of an important idea.

FOR YOUR INFORMATION

The seven important ideas of Kwanzaa are: unity, self-determination, working together, sharing, purpose, creativity, and faith. On each night of the Kwanzaa holiday, a new candle is lit to symbolize one of these seven ideas.

The light of a bonfire burns on Bonfire Night in England, also known as Guy Fawkes Day.

The Symbol of Light

A symbol that appears in the celebrations of many different groups of people is light. What does light symbolize? To answer this, think about

- the opposite of light
- the source of light in daytime
- the source of light at night

Light is a symbol that makes people feel safe and hopeful. It is used in many cultures to help decorate our homes and communities at happy times. When are lights used as decorations in your community?

During the Hindu Diwali festival, small oil lamps shine in homes and on the roofs of the buildings.

Eight candles are lit during the eight days of the Jewish Chanukah celebration. The candleholder is called a "menorah." The highest candle, called the *shammus* candle, is used to light the eight other candles.

In December some Scandinavian people celebrate the memory of an Italian woman named Saint Lucia by lighting torches. The light also cheers up people during the dark winter season.

Festivals of Light

Different groups of people have put the symbol of light into their celebrations. These celebrations are sometimes called "festivals of light." They include the ones in this chart.

Festivals of Light

Celebration	People who Started the Celebration
Bonfire Night/Guy Fawkes Day	English
Chanukah	Jewish
Christmas	Christian
Diwali	Hindu
Feast of the Lanterns	Chinese
Holi	Indian from India
Julian Christmas	Ukrainian
Kwanzaa	African-American
Now Ruz	Iraqi, Irani, Afghan
St. Lucia Day	Scandinavian
St-Jean Baptiste Day	French Canadian
Sun Dance	Native peoples

In this activity you are going to make a symbol for a festival of light.

1. Choose a festival of light to research.

2. Find facts about the festival of light. People, encyclopedias, or library books can help you.

3. Think of a symbol that shows what the festival means or makes people feel.

4. Draw the symbol and put it up with everyone else's symbols around the classroom. Write down
   – which festival of light your symbol shows
   – what your symbol means

Invite other people to take a tour of all the symbols in your classroom. Share with them what you have learned about festivals of light.

Gifts are for Giving

All of us enjoy getting gifts. We feel excited, happy, and special. How do you feel when you give a gift? Because giving and getting gifts brings so much joy to people, it is an important part of many celebrations.

Children all over the world have given and received gifts, since gifts are part of so many celebrations.

Celebrations With Gifts

During the festival of Diwali, the Hindu and Sikh people of India give each other boxes of Indian sweets. This custom is also celebrated here in Canada by Hindu and Sikh people. Maybe there is someone in your community who could tell your class about it. Maybe they will offer you some sweets!

On Eed-ul-Fitr, many Muslims celebrate the end of Ramadan. Ramadan is the ninth month of the Muslim calendar. In this month, many Muslims spend much time praying and do not eat between daybreak and sunset. Many families celebrate Eed-ul-Fitr by giving money to the poor. This celebration also includes eating special foods and sweets, and visiting family friends. Parents give gifts to their children and play games with them.

Around the end of January, many people celebrate Chinese New Year. Children get small red envelopes with money in them from their relatives. This is called "good luck money," and children can spend it any way they want to during the holiday.

An envelope from Chinese New Year to hold "good luck money"

Remember Giving a Gift

Think back to a time when you gave a gift to someone. It may have been a thing that you wrapped, or it could have been a promise to do something for someone. Think about what happened when you gave the gift. You might want to draw some pictures to help you remember clearly. Share your memories with others.

In this activity you are going to find out how people in your class have given gifts and received gifts.

1. Read the questions on the form "Gift-Giving People Search."

2. Walk around to other people and ask them if they fit the descriptions in each square of the sheet.

3. When someone fits a description, ask him or her to sign the square.

Share your stories and feelings about giving and getting gifts.

From Sea to Sea to Sea

The place where you live is an important part of your life. You share this place—its land, its seasons, its history, its people—with your neighbours. This makes you all members of a community. People have always found ways to celebrate their communities—block parties, country fairs, and summer exhibitions are a few examples. The celebrations of communities all over the country make Canada a special place to live.

A street party in Toronto, Ontario.

Picking pumpkins at the Fall Harvest Festival in Charlottetown, Prince Edward Island.

Have you ever gone to a celebration like the ones in the pictures below? Maybe your neighbourhood throws a block party every year—no cars are allowed on the street, everyone brings food, and games are organized for children. Maybe you live in or near a farming community—your neighbours celebrate the local fruits and vegetables by holding a fair with rides, car shows, and lots and lots of food. You might live in or near a big city like Toronto or Vancouver and go to the Canadian or Pacific National Exhibitions where there are rides, shows, and pavilions. Then again, you might live in a part of the country where rodeos are popular. These are only a few of the kinds of community celebrations in Canada. What community celebrations have you been to in the last year?

Crowds of people walk along the fairway at the Pacific National Exhibition in Vancouver, British Columbia.

A bull rider works with a clown at a Calgary Stampede rodeo.

One way to find out about the climate of a place is by using an atlas. The table of contents of many atlases will have sections on climate and weather.

Weather and Land Features in Celebrations

Because Canada is such a big country, many different kinds of community celebrations are held here. Have you ever thought about how huge this country really is? It is the world's second-largest country after Russia, with almost ten million square kilometres. Places in such a large area may differ from each other in many ways. For example, the weather (also called the climate) and the physical features of the land (the land's geography) are different in northern and southern Canada. Climate and geography affect the kinds of food people can grow. Climate and geography also affect the kinds of activities people do at different times of the year.

The article on page 89 about a community festival in Iqaluit, Baffin Island shows how geography and climate can affect how people celebrate.

CHECK IT OUT

Use an atlas to find
• a place in Canada that is colder in January than your community (if there is one)
• a place in Canada that is hotter in July than your community (if there is one)

Celebrating in a Cold Place

Excerpted from Owl *magazine entitled* "It's Cold Here, But It's Fun!" *by Penny Williams*

A popular event at Toonik Tyme is the blanket toss.

What would you say if you lived on Baffin Island in the Canadian Arctic and spring was coming?

"It's cold here, but it's fun!"

Why is spring such a big deal on Baffin Island? On the shortest winter days in Iqaluit, the sun is only up for three hours. In Pond Inlet, there's no sun for two months!

Most places in the Arctic have feasts and games to welcome the spring. In Iqaluit, there's a week-long celebration called Toonik Tyme. "At Toonik Tyme, we saw the fireworks, Skidoo races, and the igloo-building contest," says Jimmy, 12. There are also harpoon-throwing contests and dogsled races. To raise money for the school library in the spring, Pond Inlet has a golf game—on ice! Ashley, 10, says, "It's my first time golfing, but I think it will be fun." And it is—Ashley wins a prize for being the youngest golfer.

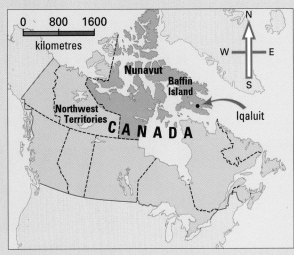

Iqaluit is one of the coldest places in Canada because it is so far north.

Celebrating in a Warmer Place

If you travel about 2600 kilometres south of Iqaluit, you reach Leamington, a town in Canada with different geography and climate, and a different kind of community celebration.

Leamington, Ontario is in the south of Canada. It has much warmer weather than Iqaluit. The weather is perfect for growing tomatoes. Tomatoes need warm, sunny weather and the right amount of rain to grow plump and juicy. Because of the excellent tomato-growing climate in Leamington, the H.J. Heinz Company opened up a food plant there. More people work at the food plant than anywhere else in town.

The tomato harvest in Leamington is a time for celebration, so the town holds a tomato festival every August. Two of the big events are a tomato race and a contest to judge the largest tomato. The tomato festival also has a farmers' market, food booths, a petting zoo, and pony rides. The festival has something for everyone: if you're interested in cars and motorcycles, there is a car show and motorcycle race. Other people might have more fun at the baby contest or the game booths.

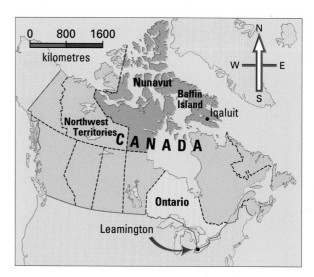

Leamington, Ontario is one of the most southern towns in Canada.

A parade at the Leamington Tomato Festival

To Do

In this activity you are going to make an ad for one of Canada's community celebrations.

1. Look at the list of Canadian community celebrations on pages 92 and 93. Choose one that interests you.

2. Try to find the community of the celebration on a map of Canada. (If you cannot find the community, find the province.)
   – What do you think the weather is like when the celebration is held?

3. Write down what you think the celebration is like.
   – What events do you think might take place?
   – What do you think are the most fun events?

4. Make an ad for this celebration. It could be
   – a poster
   – a brochure
   – a radio ad
   – any other kind of ad

Present your ads. Show how the place, the season, and the events of your celebration make it exciting!

Leamington Tomato Festival
See these great events!
• Great Tomato Race
• Largest Tomato Contest
• Tomato Festival Parade
• Petting Zoo
• Car Show

Fall

APPLEFEST

Baking contests, talent shows,
arts and crafts
Brighton, Ontario
September

Winter

WINTERLUDE

Major North American winter festival
Ottawa, Ontario
February

CARNAVAL DE QUÉBEC

Québec's fabulous winter carnival
Québec City, Québec
February

Spring

CARIBOU CARNIVAL

Canadian Championship Dog Derby
Yellowknife, Northwest Territories
March/April

WESTERN CANADA
INTERNATIONAL POW WOW

Native crafts and foods
Regina, Saskatchewan
April

CANADIAN TULIP FESTIVAL

Tons of tulips, arts and crafts
Ottawa, Ontario
May

ANNAPOLIS VALLEY
APPLE BLOSSOM FESTIVAL

Barbeques, sports, parades, and dances
Kentville, Nova Scotia
May

Summer

SHEDIAC LOBSTER FESTIVAL

"Lobster capital of the world"

Shediac, New Brunswick

July

A TASTE OF MANITOBA

A foodlover's delight

Winnipeg, Manitoba

July

CALGARY EXHIBITION AND STAMPEDE

Wild West rodeo and stampede

Calgary, Alberta

July

CANADIAN INTERNATIONAL DRAGON BOAT FESTIVAL

Chinese Dragon boat races

Vancouver, British Columbia

July

SUMMERSIDE LOBSTER CARNIVAL

Arts, crafts, and food

Summerside, Prince Edward Island

July

NEWFOUNDLAND AND LABRADOR FOLK FESTIVAL

A cultural showcase

St. John's, Newfoundland

August

DAWSON CITY DISCOVERY DAYS

Celebrate the Klondike gold discovery

Dawson City, Yukon

August

Celebrating Who We Are

What would life be like without celebrations? How would your feelings about yourself, your family, your neighbours, and your country be different?

Most of the celebrations you have learned about are very old. They have been passed down from parents to children over many years. Celebrations, whether they are religious, seasonal, or mark special events in our lives, are very important to us.

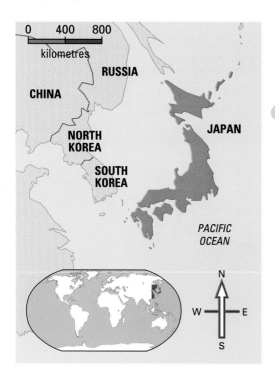

Imagine you are going to move to a faraway place where the people have customs and celebrations different from yours. Which celebration would you want to take with you? Why would you choose that celebration?

When people move to a new part of the world, they may change their celebrations. Sometimes this happens because the new place has different weather or different foods; in other cases, people want to add something from their new home to old customs.

In the following story, a woman has moved across the ocean from the United States to a new home in Japan. One day she feels a great need to bring a celebration from her old world, the United States, back into her life in Japan.

Tree of Cranes

Written and illustrated by Allen Say

When I was not yet old enough to wear long pants, Mama always worried that I might drown in a neighbour's pond. Time and again she warned me not to play there, but I never listened because the pond was filled with carp of bright colours.

The last time I went there was a grey winter day, too cold for the fish to move around. They never came out from under the rocks, and all I caught was a bad chill.

Mama would be upset with me, I knew. She would know right away how I got my mittens all wet.

But then she might be happy just to see me.

"Mama, I'm home!" I called. There was no answer.

She always met me at the porch, always. I called again, and finally she answered, sounding far away. I waited, but she didn't come out to see me. She must be sick, I thought.

Mama was in the living room, folding origami paper. She just nodded, barely looking at me. But there were two slices of my favourite tea cake waiting for me. That made me feel better.

"Why are you making cranes?" I asked.

"Because I want to make a big wish," she said without looking up.

"You're going to fold a thousand cranes to make your wish come true?"

"Maybe even two thousand . . ." She reached out and touched my face with her cool hand.

"Why, you're hot all over." Mama frowned and gave me a silent stare.

I hung my head and said nothing. She knew.

Anytime Mama thought I had a cold it was time for a hot bath.

"Ten whole minutes and not one second less," she told me.

She was upset. She didn't even rinse my back. Her slippers were shuffling all the way down the hallway. Then a door closed shut. She wasn't coming back to keep me company.

I'd better say I'm sorry, I thought to myself.

But before I could apologize, Mama put me in my nightclothes!

"I don't want to go to bed!"

"You need to stay nice and warm."

"All afternoon?"

"All afternoon."

"Will you read me stories?"

"No stories. But I'll make you hot lunch."

I knew what that meant. Rice gruel. Only sick people ate rice gruel.

And that's what I had, with a sour plum and yellow radishes, eating all alone and drinking hot tea in Papa's big cup.

Then I lay down facing the door and hoped and hoped Mama would come back with an apple and peel the skin in a long strip like a red ribbon and then read me a story.

The door never opened.

"Mama!" I called finally. She didn't answer.

After a long while I heard a noise coming from the garden. Maybe the old gardener had come to clip our trees again. I got up and opened the window.

It was snowing outside. And Mama was digging around a small tree.

"What are you doing?" I shouted.

Mama stopped and stared.

"Close that window this second and go straight back to bed!"

Quickly I closed the window and lay down again. She's really angry now, I thought. But why is she gardening in the snow? Is she digging a hole because she's angry with me? I didn't know what to think.

I was nearly asleep when Mama came in. She was carrying a tree in a blue pot. It was the little pine Mama and Papa had planted when I was born, so I would live a long life like the tree.

"What are you doing with my tree?" I asked.

"You'll see," she said, setting down the pot. "Do you know what today is?"

"Ah . . . seven days before the New Year's Day."

"That's right," she said, and smiled! Then she fetched the silver cranes and some sewing things from the living room.

Finally Mama sat down. She put a thread through one of the cranes and hung it from the tree.

"I have been acting strangely all day," she said. I started to reply, but she shushed me. "If you promise to stay in bed, I will tell you why."

"I promise," I said.

"I was born and lived far away in another country, long before I came here and met your father."

"Where?"

"A warm place called Ca-li-for-ni-a," she whispered.

I nodded.

"Today is a very special day in that warm place. If you happened to be there now, you would see trees like this everywhere, all decorated with winking lights and small globes of silver and gold . . .

"And under each tree there are boxes of presents people give to friends and loved ones."

"I want a samurai kite!" I said.

"You give and receive, child. It is a day of love and peace. Strangers smile at one another. Enemies stop fighting. We need more days like it." She put the last crane on the tree.

"It's wonderful!" I cried.

"It's not finished," she said. And she brought some candles from the kitchen and tied them to the branches.

"Are you going to burn my tree?" I asked.

Mama laughed. "Just the candles, and only for a short while. We'll replant your tree tomorrow."

"I want to light them! May I, may I?"

"Do it quickly then."

Mama let me strike the matches. And when all the candles were lit, she fell silent. She was remembering. She was seeing another tree in a faraway place where she had been small like me.

Mama held me in her lap. The cranes turned slowly, flashing candlelight. There couldn't be a tree more beautiful than mine, I thought. Not even in the place where Mama was born.

"What present would you like?" I asked.

"Only peace and quiet," Mama said.

"I mean something from me."

"Oh, something very, very special . . . like a promise."

"I said I would stay in bed."

"Another promise, then."

"All right."

"Give me your word you'll never go to the pond again."

I promised.

I was fast asleep when Papa came home.

Next morning I jumped out of bed because a fierce warrior was staring at me. But it was only a kite.

Only a kite! The one I'd always wanted! Then I saw the tree behind it, my tree. Suddenly I remembered last night and all that Mama had told me.

Thank you, Mama! Thank you, Papa!

I ran outside with my present.

Outside, everything was covered with snow.

"There'll be another day," Mama said. "A fine windy day with no snow."

"Plenty of snow to make a snowman!" Papa said. "Let's make one together."

And like the snowman we made, many years have melted away now. But I will always remember that day of peace and quiet. It was my first Christmas.

⟶

The woman in the story mixed two cultures together. What customs did she bring from her birthplace? What customs did she add from her new home?

To Do

In this activity you are going to invent a celebration that includes everyone in your class.

1. Brainstorm reasons for your class to celebrate together. Choose one for your new celebration.

2. Make a web of the parts of a celebration that you could include in your new celebration. These include
   – special clothing
   – decorations
   – food

3. Decide what parts to include in your new celebration. Make the parts of the celebration show the customs of people in your class.

Set aside a special time to share your new celebration with each other and visitors.

Generations

A generation is a group of people born about 30 years apart. You and your brothers and sisters are part of one generation. Your parents are part of another generation. Learn about what life was like for people in past generations. Look at their homes, food, work, schools, and play. Create your own museum to show others what you've learned about how people lived in the past and what you think life will be like in the future.

A STORY TO TELL

What stories have your parents told you about their childhood? What stories have they told you about their parents or grandparents? Family stories help people know where they came from and who they are.

This picture was painted by George Littlechild, an artist and an author. It tells part of his family story. Read about the picture on page 105.

George Littlechild was born in 1958. This painting is from a 1993 book he wrote about his art and his family history called *This Land Is My Land*.

I Love the Moon, the Stars, and the Ancestors

Excerpted from This Land Is My Land
by George Littlechild

I paint at night. I'm inspired to paint at night. I stand outside staring at the night sky and I begin to dream. The sky is like a doorway into the other world, the spirit world.

I am inspired by the ancestors. When I look back on our history and see all the difficulties our ancestors had to face, I can only honour them. Through the wisdom of our Elders and the courage of all our people we have survived the past 500 years. I thank the Creator for Wahkomkanak, our ancestors.

In the centre of this picture is Chief Joseph Samson. He wears an eagle headdress, the highest symbol in our culture. On the top and the sides of the picture are images of my great-great-grandfather, Louis Natuasis, who lived from 1858 to 1926. He was a headman to Chief Joseph Samson. He was born when my people were still free, when the buffalo still roamed.

In those days our Nation, the Plains Cree people, followed the buffalo in the spring and summer. In the winter we made camp by the rivers, which were the ancient roadways. The trees protected us from the snows and the winds. We hid in the valleys from our traditional enemies, the Blackfoot people.

The artist George Littlechild grew up in Alberta and now lives in British Columbia.

Showing a Family Story

There are many ways of showing a family story. George Littlechild shows his family story by painting the faces of people in his family's past. He also uses symbols like the eagle headdress. Another family picture story might show an event that happened to somebody's parent or grandparent or even great-grandparent. A family picture story could also include a map showing a journey a family took.

A family's stories are a valuable treasure. Every family decides which stories to pass on to their children. Many of these stories help children know more about how life was different for people in the past.

To Do

In this activity you are going to share a story about someone in your family's past.

1. Remember a story you have heard about someone in your family from a past generation. If you can't remember one, you could ask a family member.

2. Write down the main points.

3. Decide how to illustrate the story. You could show
   – important objects and symbols like George Littlechild did
   – an event in the person's life

Prepare your good copy and share it with others.

Working on Your Project

All through this unit, you will work on a museum exhibit. A museum exhibit shows objects and pictures about a topic. Your exhibit will show objects and pictures about life in the past.

Museums and Exhibits

Many objects in a museum are from the past. When you compare these objects to the things we have now, the differences can be surprising. You might wonder, "What would it have been like to be alive in a time when the things around me were so different? How different would my thoughts and dreams have been?" What do you wonder when you look at the pictures of exhibit objects on this page?

A phonograph from 1900. Phonographs were used for listening to music.

This kitchen exhibit from Lawrence House in Maitland, Nova Scotia shows objects from about the year 1870.

This exhibit from Black Creek Pioneer Village in Toronto, Ontario shows objects and clothing from about the year 1810.

WHAT YOU CAN PUT IN YOUR EXHIBIT

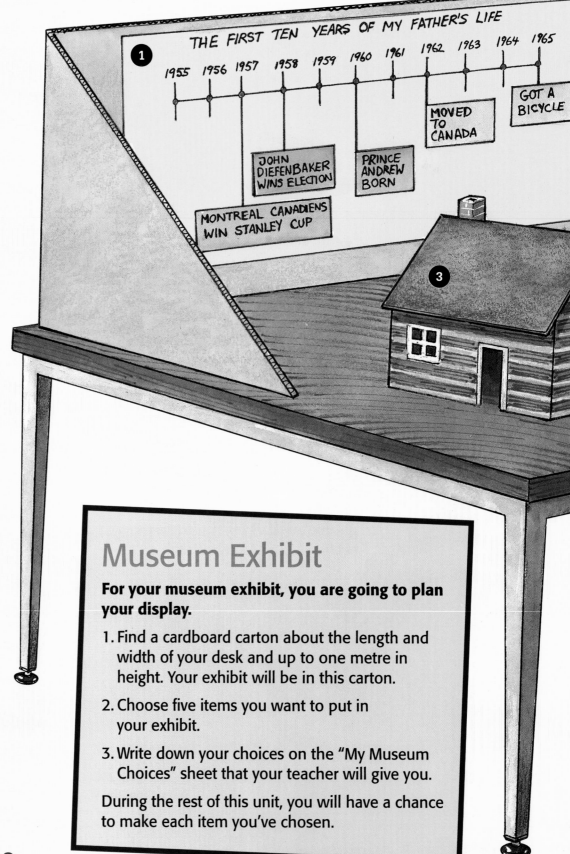

Museum Exhibit

For your museum exhibit, you are going to plan your display.

1. Find a cardboard carton about the length and width of your desk and up to one metre in height. Your exhibit will be in this carton.

2. Choose five items you want to put in your exhibit.

3. Write down your choices on the "My Museum Choices" sheet that your teacher will give you.

During the rest of this unit, you will have a chance to make each item you've chosen.

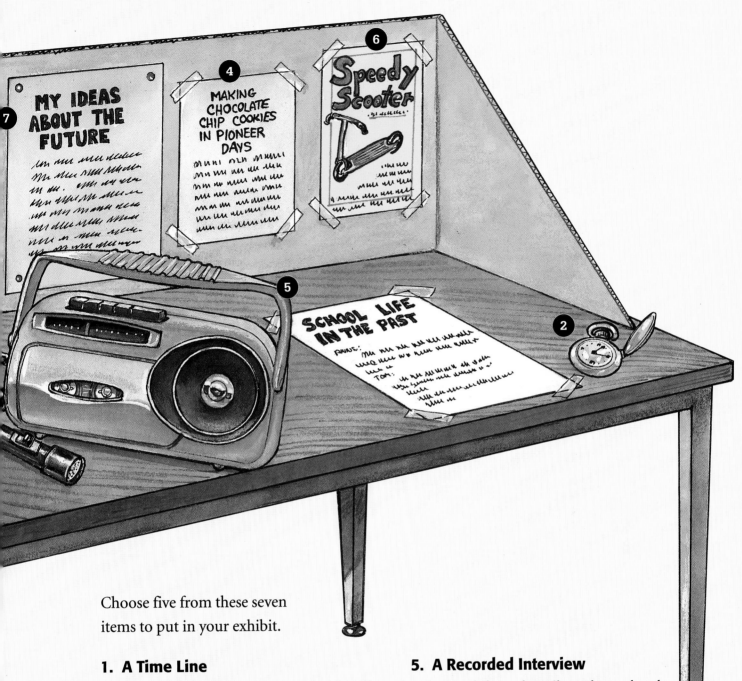

Choose five from these seven items to put in your exhibit.

1. A Time Line
Show what happened in the world and in your parents' lives when they were children.

2. An Artifact
Make or find an object from the past that could have belonged to one of your ancestors.

3. A Model of a House
Make a house from many years ago.

4. Instructions for Making Food
Write down how people in the past would have prepared your favourite food.

5. A Recorded Interview
Ask an adult to describe what school was like in a past generation.

6. An Advertisement for a Toy
Make a poster advertising a toy that a child from the past might have enjoyed.

7. Your Ideas About the Future
Show how life might change in future generations.

109

NOTCHES IN TIME

Since you've been born, many events have happened in your life and in the world. A time line is one way to list some of the things that have happened. What are the most interesting and important events that happened since you were born?

The time line at the bottom of the page starts at the year 1986 and ends at the year 1995. During these ten years, different kinds of events happened in the world. The photos show five of these events. See how the line connecting the photo to the time line shows what year the event took place.

Everyday Life
The top-selling toys in Canada were Teenage Mutant Ninja Turtle figures.

Science
Scientists found dinosaur eggs in Alberta.

1986   1987   1988   1989   1990

Politics
Jean Chrétien became Prime Minister of Canada.

Music
Celine Dion won the Juno Award for Female Vocalist of the Year for the second year in a row.

Sports
Toronto and Vancouver joined the National Basketball Association.

1991   1992   1993   1994   1995

In this activity you are going to make a time line of important events during your life.

1. Write down every year that you have been alive. Start with the year you were born.

2. List three personal events in your life. For example,
   — I moved to Canada in 1991.
   — I started piano lessons in 1995.

3. List three events that happened in the world during your lifetime.

4. You can find world events for your list by
   — asking older people in your family
   — looking through reference books called almanacs
   — looking through almanacs on CD-ROM

5. Put your personal and world events on a time line. You could add pictures to your time line to make it more interesting.

Look at each others' time lines. How many different events do they show?

Bookshelf

Almanacs are books with facts about discoveries and events. Almanacs are also in CD-ROM form. Two almanacs you can find in the reference section of your school or public library are

The Canadian Global Almanac (book) (Macmillan: Toronto, updated every year)

The Canadian Almanac and Directory (book and CD-ROM) (Canadian Almanac and Directory Publishing Company: Toronto, updated every year)

FOR YOUR INFORMATION

Many of North America's Native peoples used time lines called calendar sticks. They were made by people in the tribe called Sky Watchers or Calendar Keepers. They made marks in wooden sticks to show changes in the positions of the sun, moon, and stars. The sticks could be held upright like canes.

Working on Your Project

How big a difference do you think there is between your generation and your parents' generation? Doing an older person's time line for your museum exhibit will help you find out.

Life in the Last Generation

When your parents were children, some of their personal events were the same as yours. Other personal events in their lives were different because the world around them was different. These pictures show some events from a child's life in the 1950s. How are they different from your life?

I got hula hoops in 1958.

We got a station wagon in 1956.

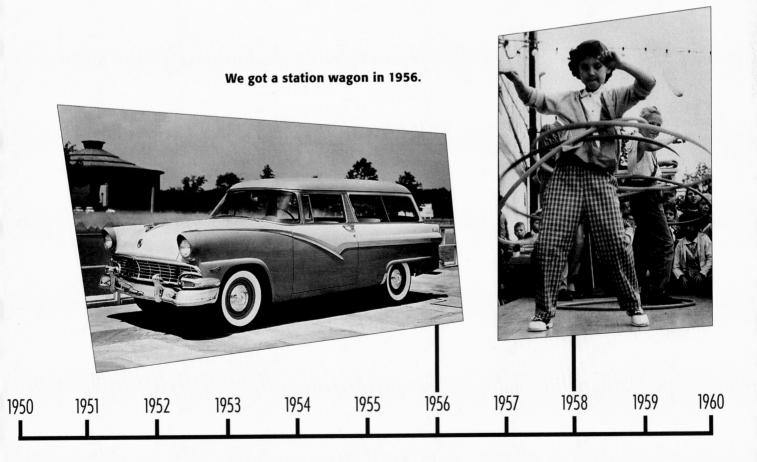

| 1950 | 1951 | 1952 | 1953 | 1954 | 1955 | 1956 | 1957 | 1958 | 1959 | 1960 |

Some Events in the Last Generation

When your parents were children, different world events were taking place. Here are three examples.

1967
Expo '67 opens in Montréal.

1969
American astronaut Neil Armstrong is the first person to walk on the moon.

1968
Canadian Nancy Greene wins the gold medal for alpine skiing at the Winter Olympics in Grenoble, France.

Museum Exhibit

For your museum exhibit, you are going to make a time line of the childhood of an older person.

1. Find an older person and ask what year he or she was born. Write down the next nine years in a list going down a page.

2. Ask the person to tell you three personal events from their childhood and when they happened.

3. Ask the person to tell you three events that happened in the world during his or her childhood and when they happened.

4. If the person cannot tell you of three events
   – ask other older people
   – look through an almanac

5. Put all the events on a time line.

How is the older person's time line different from your time line?

Life in a New Place

People move to new places for many reasons. In this story, Adam and his family move to Canada from Russia. Read the story and think about what helped Adam begin life in a new place.

The Always Prayer Shawl

by Sheldon Oberman, Illustrated by Ted Lewin

Adam was a Jewish boy in Russia many years ago. When Adam went for eggs, he did not get them from a store. He got them from a chicken.

When Adam felt cold, he did not turn a dial for heat. He chopped wood for a fire. When Adam went to town, he did not ride in a car. He rode in a wagon pulled by a horse.

Adam did not go to a big school. He went to his grandfather's house. There his grandfather taught all the children the stories of their people and how to read and write in Hebrew. All this was special to Adam, but most special of all was Adam's name.

One day Adam asked his grandfather, "Why is my name Adam?" His grandfather rubbed his beard and smiled. He took Adam to the synagogue, and they sat by the window. Adam shut his eyes and felt the warm sun shining on his face.

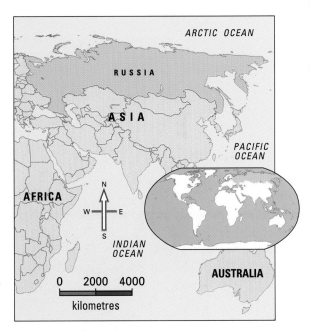

115

Then his grandfather answered, "You are named after my grandfather whose name was Adam. He was named after his grandfather's grandfather whose name was Adam. That way there will always be an Adam."

Adam laughed and whispered into his grandfather's ear, "I am always Adam. That won't change!"

"Aha!" said his grandfather. "Some things change. And some things don't."

Then many things began to change. There was trouble in Russia. There was not enough food. People were hungry. Soldiers were fighting everywhere. Everyone was afraid.

Adam's parents said, "We must leave our home and go to a better place. It is so far away that we can never come back." Adam's grandfather said, "You must go without me. I am too old to change anymore." Adam cried, "I don't want to leave you, Grandfather! I will never see you again!"

Adam's grandfather kissed him for the last time. He held out his prayer shawl and he said, "My grandfather gave me this prayer shawl. Now I am giving it to you." Adam held it tightly against his chest. He could hardly speak for his tears, so he whispered, "I am always Adam and this is my always prayer shawl. That won't change."

Off they went. Adam and his family travelled for weeks. They came to a town by the sea and got on a ship and sailed for weeks.

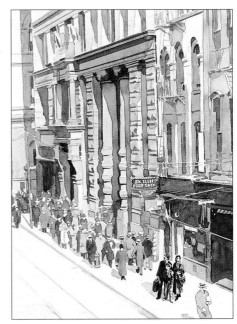

They came to a new country where everyone spoke a different language and wore different clothes. Things changed even more. They moved into a small apartment in a big city. Adam's parents went to work in a factory. Adam went to school and learned English, science, and history. Everything felt different except for the prayer shawl. Every Saturday Adam put on the prayer shawl and he said, "I am always Adam and this is my Always Prayer Shawl. That won't change."

Other things kept changing. Adam grew up and he married. He worked in a store from morning until night. Still, every Saturday Adam put on his prayer shawl. Finally, the fringes wore out. So he sewed on new ones.

Then Adam had children. He moved to a house at the edge of the city. He drove back each day to work in an office. Still, every Saturday Adam put on his prayer shawl. Finally, the collar wore out. So he sewed on a new one.

Then Adam's children grew up. They moved out. They married and had children of their own. Adam and his wife grew very old, and they went to live in a home with other old people. Still, every Saturday Adam put on his prayer shawl. Finally, the cloth wore out. So he sewed on a new one.

One day, Adam's grandson came to visit. "Grandfather," the grandson asked, "Were you ever a kid like me?" Adam rubbed his beard and smiled. He said, "I was like you and I was not like you. I got eggs from a chicken, not from a store. I chopped wood for heat, I did not turn a dial. I rode in a wagon pulled by a horse, and not in a car. And I didn't go to a big school. I went to a little house where my grandfather taught me many things."

The grandson asked, "What did he teach you?" Adam took out his prayer shawl. He said, "Put this on. Maybe I can teach you something that he taught me." Adam's grandson put on the prayer shawl.

They went to the synagogue, and they sat by the window. They shut their eyes and felt the warm sun shining on their faces.

Adam said, "This prayer shawl belonged to my grandfather. Before that, it belonged to his grandfather whose name was also Adam. Now it is mine. And someday I will give it to you. It has changed many times. The fringes changed. The collar changed. The cloth changed. Everything about it has changed. But it is still my Always Prayer Shawl. It is just like me. I have changed and changed and changed. But I am still Adam."

Adam's grandson whispered into his ear, "I am going to be just like you. I will have a grandson whose name will be Adam. And someday I will give him this Always Prayer Shawl."

"Aha!" said Adam. "Now I can teach you something that my grandfather taught me. He taught me that some things change and some things don't."

Talk about these questions with your classmates:
• What were some of the everyday things that Adam and his family would have found challenging in their new land?
• By the time the prayer shawl wore out, Adam could probably have afforded to buy a beautiful new one. Why didn't he?

THE CHALLENGES OF MOVING TO CANADA

These days it is still hard to leave one home behind and move to a new land. Some of the hardships of moving to Canada for the first time are described by the young people in the pictures below.

I was born in India and arrived in Canada last January. Something I found hard about living in Canada is staying warm in the winter. In India, the temperature is usually much higher than 20°C.

I had a problem learning English at school. It took me a long time, and it was hard to talk when nobody understood. Sometimes I had to show what I meant with my hands.

I felt lonely a lot when I came to Canada. It was hard to make new friends, even if some people were nice to me.

It was a little hard to get used to Canadian cooking. In Korea, we ate rice with every meal, and we used chopsticks. Even though we still eat Korean food with chopsticks at home, the food in school and in stores and restaurants is very different.

School was hard for me at first. In my country, we started school at seven o'clock in the morning and we learned about industrial arts and gardening. We didn't have as many class discussions as Canadian schoolchildren do. Sometimes I can't think of anything to say.

In this activity you are going to perform a skit about the challenges faced by people coming to live in Canada.

1. In a group, choose a challenge. It could be
   — one of the challenges on pages 18 or 19
   — another challenge that your group thinks of

2. Plan your skit to show
   — a newcomer going through the challenge
   — how the newcomer and other people can help with the challenge

3. Practise your skit.

4. Present your skit to the rest of the class.

Discuss what each skit was about.

Working on Your Project

An artifact is something made by people, like the prayer shawl in the story on pages 115 to 119. Natural objects, like rocks, are not artifacts. Artifacts are often found in museum exhibits to show life in the past.

CHECK IT OUT

What are some other examples of artifacts in and around your school? What are some examples of objects which are not artifacts?

The Stories Behind Artifacts

People can become very attached to artifacts. They may bring them along when they move to new places and pass them on to their children. Imagine the stories artifacts could tell if they could speak. A shawl or quilt could tell about all the changes that took place in its long life. Here are two examples of artifacts sharing the changes they have been through.

The Story of a Mortar and Pestle

What a change in my life! I remember when I lived in the jungles of Burma. It seems we were always on the run. But wherever we were, my job was most important. My owners were rebels living and hiding in the jungle. My owner had a little baby girl. She was born right there in the jungle. When she was old enough to eat food, they used me to mash it up. I was so proud. When they came to Canada they brought me with them. Now they use me to grind garlic and other delicious ingredients. But I still remember the good old days!

The Story of a Cedar Box

I have always been special to my owners. Five generations ago, my maker built me from a cedar tree. I stored food such as dried meat, dried fish, and a hard biscuit called hardtack. After many years of service, my maker's great-grandson painted an eagle on my lid. My new owner makes totem poles for the Tsimshian (TSIM-she-un) Native peoples in British Columbia. He uses me to store his carving tools. I love watching his face light up when he opens me. I know he can still smell the foods I used to hold. I can tell he treasures the memories of the past that I bring him.

Museum Exhibit

For your museum exhibit, you are going to find or make an artifact and write a story about it.

1. Choose an artifact from your family's past. For example,
   — a tool
   — a piece of clothing
   — an album

2. Prepare the artifact.
   — If your family gives you permission, bring an artifact from home.
   — If you cannot bring an artifact from home, imagine what an artifact from another generation might have looked like. Make a model of it or draw a picture of it.

3. Write a story of the artifact's life from the artifact's point of view.

Add your artifact and story to your museum exhibit.

Home Sweet Home

Think about the different rooms in your home. They probably include a bedroom, a bathroom, a kitchen, and a room for watching TV or relaxing. Many homes 200 years ago had only one room. How did families live in such homes?

An early pioneer family might have lived in a home like this for many years. It took that long for the family to settle, grow crops, and build a barn for grain and animals.

Houses were dark inside because there was no glass for windows. If a hole for a window had been cut out, it was covered with paper, cloth, or an animal hide that was covered in oil. This allowed some light to shine through it.

Settlers had to go outside to get water and wash. They would use a nearby stream or they would dig a well. The top of the well was covered with a board or built up with stones so that no one would fall in.

A SETTLER'S FIRST HOME, 1800

Settlers' first homes were usually made of wooden logs. The spaces between logs were stuffed with moss, leaves, mud, and wood chips to keep out the wind and rain. The roof was made of pieces of tree bark and logs or straw thatch.

Some homes had planks built over the ceiling beams. This would make an attic or loft above the main floor.

The fireplace was used for cooking and heating. Sometimes a seat was built right into the fireplace so that people could enjoy the heat of the fire when the weather was very cold. The fireplace was made of stone or mud.

Early homes usually had only one room. The floor was usually covered with wooden planks. Sometimes rag rugs were placed on it. Cabins with dirt floors were cold in the winter and muddy in the spring.

Early homes did not have much furniture. Tree trunks, wooden crates, and barrels were used to make chairs and tables. Bunk beds were built right into the walls with mattresses made of tree boughs or straw. Pegs and shelves were also built into the walls.

Early settlers had to make their clothes at home. A spinning wheel would turn wool from sheep into yarn which was then dyed into different colours. The yarn was woven into cloth on a loom. Then the cloth was sewn into clothing.

Cree Homes Many Years Ago

Years ago, many Cree people camped at different places in different seasons of the year. One type of home at a campsite was called a migwam.

A CREE HOME, 1800

Cree people had many different jobs to do each season. They had to fish, hunt, and pick berries for food. They also had to make hunting and cooking tools, cooking pots, canoes, and clothing.

Story-telling was also an important part of people's lives: elders passed on stories about life in the past and about heroes and their adventures. People also celebrated on special occasions with drums and dancing.

Migwams had one room. The floor was covered with spruce branches, which were soft to sleep on and had a very nice smell. A fire pit was made in the centre of the floor.

The Cree women of James Bay built migwams using wooden poles tied together at the top with tree roots. These frames were covered with bark, moss, and animal skins. In the wintertime, when the people moved to another place to hunt, the outer covering was taken off and used as a toboggan cover. The frame would stay where it was, to be used again when people returned to the campsite.

The Cree built a separate migwam for cooking. In this migwam, meat hunted in the summertime was dried on a rack so that it wouldn't spoil or go bad. After a day or two of drying, the meat was hard and could be stored to be eaten in winter.

Each migwam had two openings. One was a side opening for the door which was made of an animal skin. The other was an opening at the top of the migwam to let out smoke from the fire inside.

To Do

In this activity you are going to compare your home with a home in the past.

1. Write a paragraph or draw pictures to compare your home with the early settler or the Cree home.

2. Think about these questions to get ideas. Compared to a home from long ago
   — How is your home kept warm?
   — How is your home lighted?
   — Where do people eat, sleep, work, and keep their belongings?
   — What kinds of decorations and furniture does your home have?
   — What are the roof, walls, and floor of your home made of?

In what ways would you like to live like the settlers or Cree people did many years ago?

Working on Your Project

Many generations ago, your ancestors lived in a home of some kind. What do you think it was like? Do you think it was made of wood, sod, animal skins, adobe, or stone? Your exhibit could include a model of a house from the past.

Mud-Brick Houses

Mud bricks, sometimes called adobe, have been used to build houses in places with hot, dry weather (parts of Central America, South America, Africa, and Arabic-speaking countries). Adobe is made by mixing mud with chopped straw to form bricks. The bricks are baked in the sun. Mud bricks keep houses cool inside. The mud bricks are sometimes whitewashed to reflect the sun's heat, to make the houses even cooler.

A mud-brick house from the 1800s in Zaire, Africa

Stone Houses

Some people in countries with rocky areas (Canada, European countries, India, China, Israel, and some Arabic-speaking countries) lived in stone houses. The roofs were flat or slanted. Slanted roofs were made of straw, slate tiles, or baked clay called terra cotta.

A stone house from the 1800s in Yemen, Asia

Museum Exhibit

For your museum exhibit, you are going to make a model of a house from the past.

1. Choose one of the following houses to use for your model:
   — a house your ancestors lived in many years ago
   — one of the houses on pages 124 to 129

2. Find materials that are the same as or similar to the materials used to build the house from the past.

3. Make your model.

Add your model to your museum exhibit.

Tech Tools

What materials are your home and the homes of your classmates made of? Each person in your class could find out the material used to build their homes and then you could make a master list together. You could graph the results using a computer graphing program.

CHOW DOWN!

Who does most of the cooking in your home? If you have watched people cook, you can probably make a list of the tools they use the most. These items might not have been invented yet when your great-great-grandparents were alive.

Settlers long ago made all sorts of food without depending on grocery stores or electrical appliances. They used tools and objects like the ones on these pages.

To Do

In this activity you are going to figure out the names and uses of pioneer kitchen tools.

1. Read the recipes on this page and the next.

2. For each blue word in a recipe, think about how it is used and what it might look like.

3. Match each blue word with a numbered object on page 130 or 131. Try to give reasons for your matches.

Check your answers on page 134.

ROAST CHICKEN

1. Pluck a chicken.

2. Put it on a spit in front of the fireplace.

3. Turn the spit so that all sides of the chicken are evenly cooked.

FISH SOUP

1. Pick some thyme and let it dry for a few days.

2. Catch some fish.

3. Boil the fish in a pot of water. Hang the pot on a low rung on the trammel. Attach the trammel to the crane. Swing the crane over the fire.

4. Put the dried thyme into a mortar and crush it very fine with a pestle. Add it to the pot.

5. Let the soup simmer at a lower heat by raising the pot to a higher rung on the trammel.

BREAD

1. Make bread dough by mixing together flour, fat, sugar, salt, milk, water, and boiled hop flowers.

2. Put the dough into a dough box for a few hours to give it time to rise.

3. Make a fire in the floor of the bake oven.

4. Put the loaf on a peel and slide it into the bake oven.

5. After baking, take it out of the bake oven with the peel.

JOHNNY CAKE

1. Mix flour and cornmeal with butter, an egg, sugar, milk, salt, and baking soda.

2. Put the mixture into a spider.

3. Put the spider over hot coals. Cover the spider to bake the mixture.

BUTTER

1. Milk the cow.

2. Let the milk stand in a bucket in a cool place for one or two days. The cream in the milk will rise to the top.

3. Take the cream and put it into a churn.

4. Sit by the churn and move the dasher up and down to mix the cream until small firm pieces start to float in it. These firm pieces are butter.

5. Take out the butter, wash it in cold water, and put it into a burl bowl.

6. Squeeze out the liquid in the butter by squishing it against the side of the burl bowl with a paddle.

7. Put the butter into a butter mould to shape it into a block.

CHECK IT OUT

Look up the word "burl" in the dictionary. How do you think a burl bowl was made?

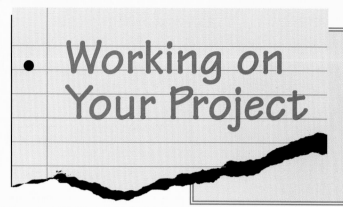

Working on Your Project

Making meals took much longer in the 1800s compared with today. Cooks did not have electric tools and could not take any shortcuts. Your exhibit could show the steps for preparing food long ago.

Getting Food in the 1800s

Families in the 1800s got most of their food from animals, farms, gardens, and the wilderness. They did not go to the grocery store for milk, cheese, and butter. Instead, they milked a cow and made their own cheese and butter. They also made their own flour.

Making Flour

To make flour, families planted wheat. When the wheat grew into stalks, they cut the stalks and beat them with a tool called a flail. This made it easy to pick out the parts of the wheat called the heads. The heads of wheat were then put on a tray and shaken hard outside in the wind. The wind would blow away the part of the wheat called chaff. The part left on the tray was called grain. The grain was poured into a quern. Someone would turn the quern's handle so that the top stone of the quern would grind the grain between the top and bottom stones. The grinding turned the grain into flour.

ANSWERS FROM PAGES 130 TO 133

1. dough box	9. spider
2. bake oven	10. churn
3. fireplace	11. dasher
4. peel	12. burl bowl
5. spit	13. paddle
6. crane	14. butter mould
7. trammel	15. mortar
8. pot	16. pestle

A quern for grinding grain. Querns were also called hand mills.

Museum Exhibit

For your museum exhibit, you are going to describe how you think a pioneer family would make your favourite food.

1. Choose your favourite food.

2. Write down the steps you need to get your favourite food today.

3. Look at your list and decide whether you think people long ago could get this food in the same way.

4. Change or add to the steps so that they could be followed by someone from the past. For information and examples,
   — see the recipes on pages 132 and 133
   — see the information on page 134
   — see a library book

5. Draw a picture to show one or more of the steps.

Add your steps and picture to your museum exhibit.

Bookshelf

These two books have helpful information on how food was made in the past.

Food for the Settler
by Bobbie Kalman (Crabtree: Niagara-on-the-Lake, 1982)

The Kitchen
by Bobbie Kalman (Crabtree: Niagara-on-the-Lake, 1990)

How To

Get Information From Books

Books are a very important source of information on the past.

• Decide what you want to find out about.

• Choose the key words. A key word is a name of a person, place, or thing that describes what you want to find out about.

• At the library, look up the key words in the subject catalogue.

• Write down the call numbers of two or three books under the key word in the subject catalogue.

• Find the books on the library shelves.

• Take the books to a quiet place in the library and look through them to see if they are helpful.

• Start writing down key words and phrases about your subject. Only write the key points. There is no need to write sentences. These are just rough notes.

SCHOOL DAYS, SCHOOL DAYS

People can tell us a lot about the past. Of course, if we want to find out about the long-ago past, there isn't anyone still alive to tell us. Instead, we can read the diaries and letters they left behind. In the letter below, 10-year-old Emma Pritchard writes about her school days.

Pritchard's Farm,
Green Lake,
Saskatchewan
Thursday, Nov. 19, 1885

Dear Meg,

Papa is going to hitch the horse up to the cutter tomorrow so Mama can go over to visit your family. Mama has already had scarlet fever so she will not catch it from you.

Arthur and I are getting up when it is still very dark these days. Arthur has to help Papa with the animals and bring in the wood while I milk the cow and churn the butter or help with the little ones. Walking to school in the deep snow is so unpleasant. I envy Sarah Fletcher gliding over the snow in her tiny cutter—even if it is pulled by a silly old nanny goat!

Last Friday we girls got to work on our samplers. I have now stitched all the letters of the alphabet.

On Monday, Peter Payne was late for school and it was his week to start the fire. We were all so cold that we had to leave our coats and mittens on until recess.

Mr. Barrett sat so close to the stove last Thursday that his pants got scorched. We could smell the cloth burning, but no one dared to laugh except Joseph. Mr. Barrett made him stand on a block of wood at the front of the class.

Last Friday we had our usual spelling match. As my team lined up against the wall, I noticed that I had more students from the younger grades on my team. I was sure we would be defeated, but it was not so. Our team won! We were so excited. I love spelling matches.

Next week I will be using Arthur's reader. Our group has finished reciting the Third Reader so we are going to use the Fourth. Arthur's is the only copy so we will all have to share. He got it from our cousins in Regina. Arthur is so big now that he can barely fit behind our small desks.

I do hope that my letter finds you feeling much better.

Your very dear friend,
Emma Pritchard

Samplers were cloth squares. Girls stitched the alphabet and simple words and sayings on them.

School Life in the 1800s

School buildings, students, and school supplies were different in the 1800s compared with today. Read about some differences below.

School Buildings

In the 1800s, schools had no blackboards, no bulletin boards, and only a few books. They had wooden walls, a wooden ceiling, and a floor of wooden planks. The only warm place in the room in the wintertime was next to the stove. Students sat at rough, uncomfortable wooden desks or tables.

Students

Emma Pritchard went to school with children of all ages. In one room, a teacher would have to teach children from the age of six all the way up to teenagers 16 or 17 years old. Often, the older students were newcomers to Canada who were learning English. They might have had to sit with younger students and use their readers to learn English.

School Supplies

Emma's reader was handed down from her older brother. In those days, there were not many materials or supplies for students to work with. Students wrote on slates, which were like small chalkboards. They used chalk or slate pencils. Books like readers were precious and had to be shared. The Bible was also used for reading practice.

To Do

In this activity you are going to make a time capsule of your school life. A time capsule is a container filled with objects.

1. In a group, collect objects and draw pictures that tell about your school life. They could show
   — what the school looks like
   — the supplies you use
   — the subjects you learn

2. Write a letter to someone from the future that explains what the objects are.

3. Put the letter and the objects in a container that can be tightly closed.

4. Discuss with the class where to put your time capsules. You might arrange to store them in a special place in the school.

Students from a future class will learn about your school life when they open your time capsule.

For Your Information

The first time capsule was buried in the grounds of the New York World's Fair in 1939. It was a torpedo-sized metal tube made by the Westinghouse Corporation. The tube was filled with microfilm, newsreels, and other objects. It is to be unearthed in A.D. 6939, five thousand years after it was buried.

Working on Your Project

Older people can tell you a great deal about what school life was like when they were young. An interview with an older person about school in the past would be an interesting part of your museum exhibit.

Museum Exhibit

For your museum exhibit, you are going to interview an older person about his or her school life.

1. Make a list of questions to ask about school life in the past.

2. Find an older person who will agree to an interview. Explain your project.

3. Interview the person.

4. Write up the interview in neat, clear sentences.

Add the interview to your museum exhibit.

How To
Interview a Person

The following steps will help you interview someone:

• Practise your interview with a classmate.

• At the start of the interview, welcome the person you are interviewing.

• During the interview, write down key ideas or statements the person makes. Don't worry about spelling. You will have a chance to check it after the interview.

• If you have trouble understanding what the person is saying, ask questions.

• Look right at the person you are interviewing to show you are interested.

• At the end of the interview, thank the person you interviewed.

FUN! FUN! FUN!

How do you think the things you use for fun would seem to children who lived over a hundred years ago? Would you enjoy playing with toys from the past? How have toys changed over the years?

On the next three pages, imaginary children from the past and present describe their favourite play objects.

This is a velocipede. I like riding on it, even though it is scary to sit so high. I cannot ride it on public streets because I have not gotten my badge from velocipede school.

This is a bicycle. The frame is made of steel, and the tires are rubber filled with air. The seat has foam rubber in it. I can change gears so that I can go up and down hills without changing how hard I pedal.

My brother and I are watching a magic lantern show. I put a glass slide in front of the candle that is burning in the magic lantern box. The light shines through the slide and makes the picture look very big on the wall. The picture above shows what a magic lantern box would look like inside.

My family and I are watching TV. For the TV to work, a machine changes sound and pictures into electrical signals. The signals travel over long distances to the TV. A receiver inside the TV set changes the electrical signals back into pictures and sound.

Tech Tools

What are the favourite TV shows of you and your classmates? You could use a computer graphing program to graph how many people like the same shows.

These are my stilts. I step onto the foot ledge and hold the hand pole. To walk, I move my right arm in the same direction and at the same time as I move my right leg. Then I move the same way with my left arm and leg.

These are my in-line skates. They are like boots with wheels. I can move very fast on them. I practise in empty parking lots away from people and other traffic.

In this activity you are going to describe a modern-day toy to a child from long ago.

1. In a group of three, decide what object you will present.

2. Describe the object. You could talk about
   — how it works
   — why you enjoy it

3. Present your object to another group as if the people in the group were children from the past.

What would children long ago think of your modern-day toys?

Working on Your Project

Children long ago did not play only with homemade toys and games. When toy makers started making toys to sell to settler families, they needed a way to tell the families about the toys. They often used advertisements in catalogues to sell their toys. An example is shown on page 145. You could make a toy advertisement from the past for your museum exhibit.

Museum Exhibit

For your museum exhibit, you are going to make an advertisement for a toy from the past.

1. Choose a toy from the past. It could be one of the toys on pages 141 to 143 or another toy.

2. Find out about the toy by
   - asking an older person
   - looking up the key word "toy" in a library subject catalogue

3. Decide on the toy's most interesting features.

4. Make an advertisement that shows the toy's features and makes people want to buy it.

Add your advertisement to your museum exhibit.

Bookshelf

Here are three books with lots of helpful information on toys and games from the past.

Early Pleasures and Pastimes
by Bobbie Kalman
(Crabtree: Niagara-on-the-Lake, Ontario, 1983)

Games From Long Ago
by Bobbie Kalman
(Crabtree: Niagara-on-the-Lake, Ontario, 1995)

Old-Time Toys
by Bobbie Kalman & David Schimpky
(Crabtree: Niagara-on-the-Lake, Ontario, 1995)

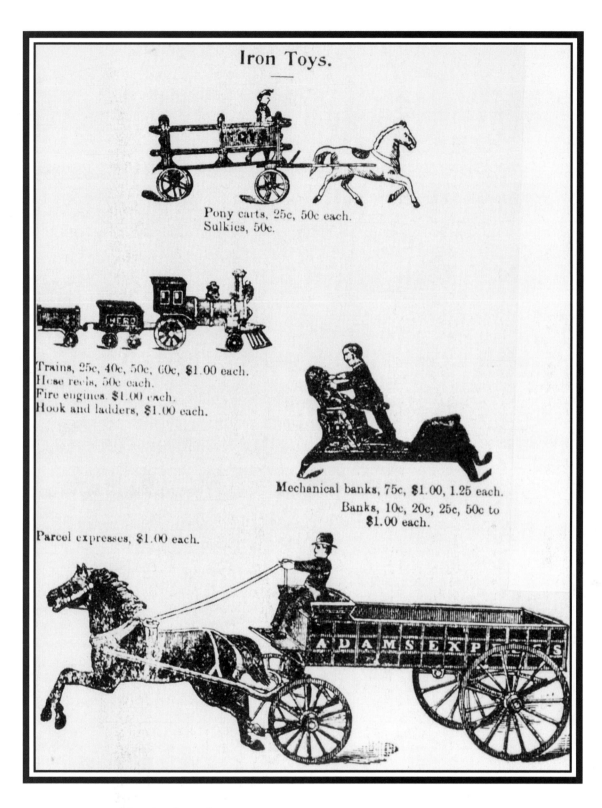

Iron Toys.

Pony carts, 25c, 50c each.
Sulkies, 50c.

Trains, 25c, 40c, 50c, 60c, $1.00 each.
Hose reels, 50c each.
Fire engines, $1.00 each.
Hook and ladders, $1.00 each.

Mechanical banks, 75c, $1.00, 1.25 each.

Banks, 10c, 20c, 25c, 50c to
$1.00 each.

Parcel expresses, $1.00 each.

**This page from the
Eaton's catalogue of
1894 to 1895 shows how
toys were advertised
over 100 years ago.**

Blast From the Past

People have always dreamed about the future. They make guesses, or predictions, about what life will be like. Sometimes the predictions come true. Sometimes the predictions are very wrong.

Read the four predictions about the future on this page and the next three pages.

City of the Future

In 1894, King Camp Gillette guessed that, in the future, most people in North America would live in one large community near Niagara Falls called Metropolis. There would be 40 000 steel-framed apartment towers in Metropolis. Groups of about 20 of these towers would be built around atriums. Atriums were large circular halls topped with glass skylights.

This picture shows what King Camp Gillette in 1894 thought a city of the future would look like.

House of the Future

In 1927, Buckminster Fuller made this model of a home of the future called the Dymaxion House. It would not weigh very much, so that the houses could be stacked on top of each other to make an apartment building.

The Mast

The most important part of the house would be the central tube-like mast made out of aluminum. The mast would contain two bathrooms and a kitchen. It would have features such as a laundry machine that could wash and dry clothes in three minutes, a garbage disposal, an electric generator, and air temperature control. Metal cables from the top of the mast would hold up the glass and plastic walls and rubber floors.

This picture shows what Buckminster Fuller in 1927 thought a house of the future would look like.

Building the House

The Dymaxion House would not be built from the ground up like houses today. Instead, an airship would carry the house to wherever people wanted to live. The airship would first drop a bomb on the site to make a large hole. The house's mast would be planted in the hole like a tree. Concrete could then be poured into the base to make the house stand up straight and steady.

Kitchen of the Future

This kitchen of the future was designed in 1944. Glass is used for the cabinet doors and for the oven. Electric appliances like waffle irons and mixers are built into the counters. The countertop is very low to the ground since people in the future will always be sitting when they prepare food. The stove and sink have hinged tops that can be closed to hide them, so that the kitchen can turn into a family or recreation room.

This picture shows what people at the Libbey-Owens-Ford company in 1944 thought a kitchen of the future would look like.

School of the Future

At the end of the 1800s, this collector card was published in France. The people who published the card guessed that in the year 2000, a teacher would feed books into a machine that would change book information into energy. The information energy would travel through wires to special helmets. When the students put on the helmets, the information would go right into their brains.

This picture shows what people at a card publishing company in the 1800s thought a classroom of the future would look like.

In this activity you are going to judge these ideas about the future that were formed in the past.

1. Join one of four groups to discuss City of the Future, House of the Future, Kitchen of the Future, or School of the Future.

2. Discuss these questions in your groups:
   — What parts of the predictions came true?
   — What parts did not come true?
   — Why do you think some of the predictions were wrong?

Present your findings to the rest of the class.

Working on Your Project

Your museum exhibit so far shows life in the past. Life has clearly changed over the years. Our homes are different, our ways of making food are different, our school life is different, and our ways of having fun are different. What kinds of changes do you think will happen in the next 100 years?

Museum Exhibit

For your museum exhibit, you are going to present your own ideas about life in the future.

1. Think about how life might be different in the future. How would these be different?
   — homes
   — food
   — school
   — fun

2. Write down your ideas about how life will change.

3. Draw one or more pictures to show your ideas.

Add your ideas and pictures to your exhibit.

Planning an Open House

After you have finished your museum exhibit, plan an open house with your class. Think about what you will say to visitors who come to see your work. Write your notes down. In them you can explain the items you have included and why you picked them. You might want to write your notes on small cards.

Your class museum is a valuable collection. It honours and respects the way people lived many generations ago. It also looks ahead with bright ideas to the way people might live in generations to come.

City or Country?

How would you describe where you live? Do you live in a busy, crowded city? Or do you live in a rural community—for example, on a farm with no neighbour in sight? Look at the following chart and think about what you would add to it.

In rural communities...	In urban communities...
• children usually live in homes farther apart	• children usually live in homes closer together
• some children take buses to school	• some children walk to school
• children might play in woods or fields	• children often play in parks or schoolyards
• some children drink water that comes from a well	• children drink water that comes through a pipe system
• some children eat food from their family's land	• children eat mostly food brought to stores by trucks
• some families make a living from farming, fishing, or hunting	• many families make a living from work in factories, offices, restaurants, hotels, or stores
• some children travel to urban communities for hospitals, movies, or museums	• some children travel to rural communities for camping, fishing, or boating

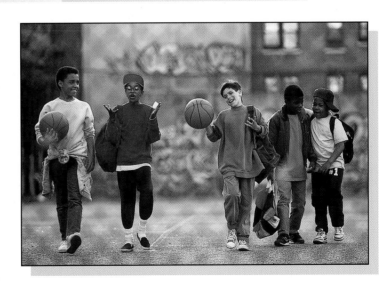

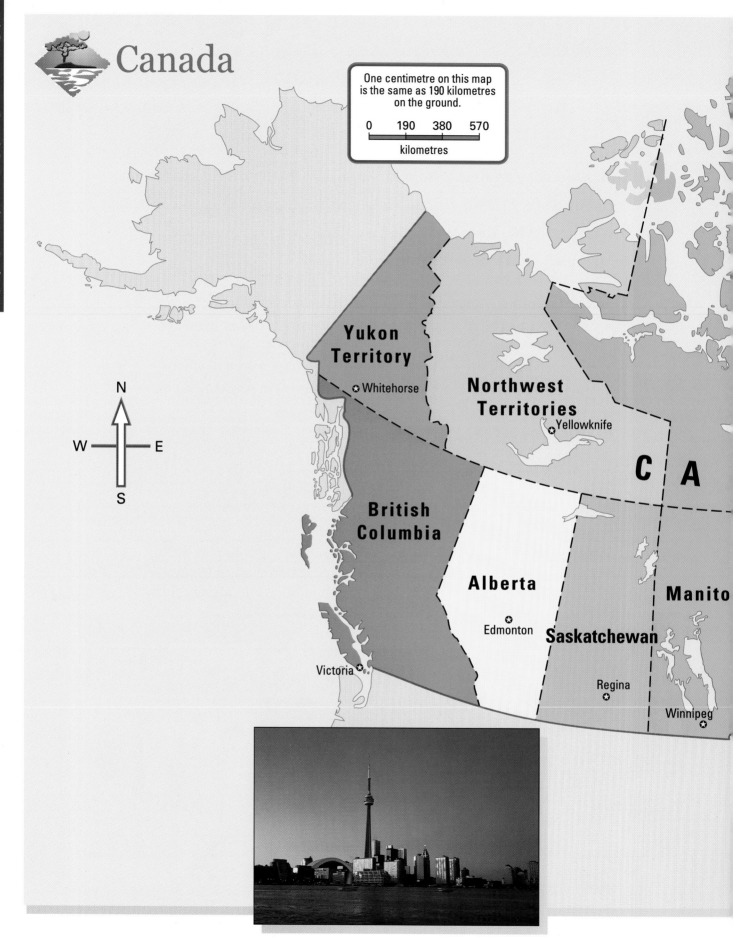

Canada

One centimetre on this map is the same as 190 kilometres on the ground.

0   190   380   570

kilometres

N
W — E
S

Yukon Territory

✪ Whitehorse

Northwest Territories

✪ Yellowknife

C A

British Columbia

Alberta

✪ Edmonton

Saskatchewan

Manito

Victoria ✪

Regina
✪

Winnipeg
✪

Toronto

Iqaluit

unavut

A D A

Newfoundland

St. John's

Québec

Ontario

Québec

P.E.I.
Charlottetown

New
Brunswick

Nova
Scotia

Fredericton

Halifax

Ottawa

Toronto

Halifax

Buying and Selling With Other Provinces

When you think about what people across Canada grow, make, or sell, what do you think of? Potatoes in P.E.I.? Oil in Alberta? Apples in Ontario?

Canadians grow, make, and sell a lot of different products and services. Many of these products and services are sold to other Canadians.

What types of things do you think Ontario buys and sells? Take a look at the products and services in these illustrations and photographs for some answers.

Ontario Buys

mineral fuels

metals

transportation services

food

ON

Ontario farm

154

Car production in southern Ontario

Ontario Sells

 transportation products

computer equipment

 telecommunications equipment

 wholesale, communication, business, and financial services

ARIO

Logging truck on Ontario highway

155

Step Into Canada's History

During a family camping trip in 1997, 12-year-old Cohen Langerak discovered a piece of Canadian history. He found a rusty lock on the shores of Lake Temiskaming. The lock had a fleur-de-lis emblem. About 350 years ago, Jesuit missionaries brought the lock from France.

Heritage Museums

Most of us don't dig up treasures from Canadian history. By visiting Canada's heritage museums, however, we can step back in time.

Upper Canada Village, near Morrisburg, is one Ontario heritage museum. It shows life in a pioneer village in the 1860s. When the St. Lawrence Seaway was being built, old settlements along the riverbanks were flooded. To save pieces of Ontario history, many buildings, machines, and furniture were moved to safety before the flooding. Later Upper Canada Village was built.

Look at the map opposite to see what a pioneer village in Upper Canada included—farms, mills, shops, and more!

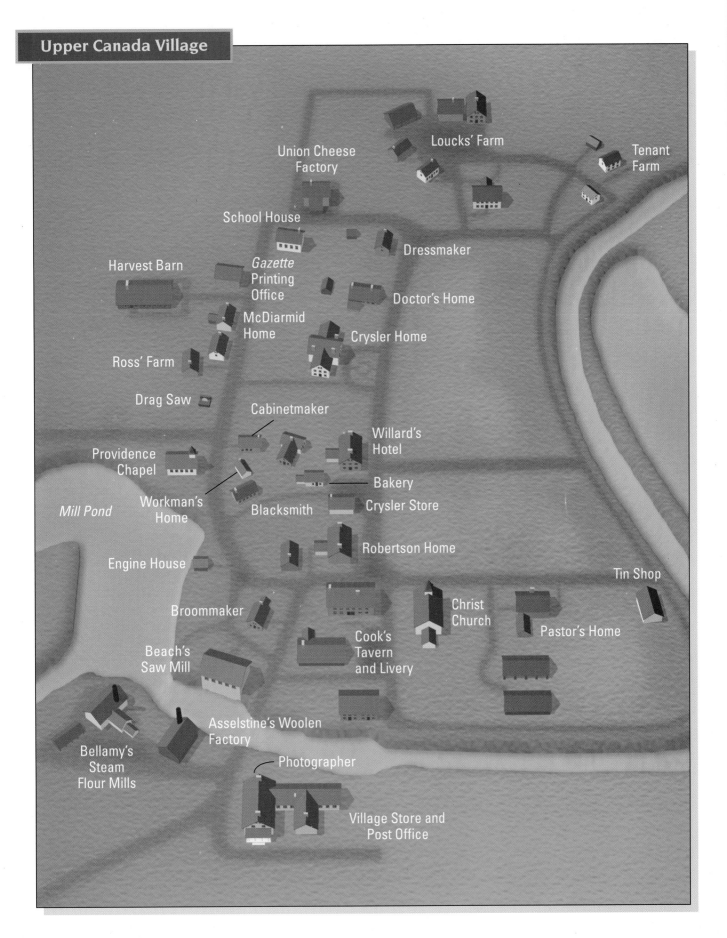

Upper Canada Village

Loucks' Farm

Tenant Farm

Union Cheese Factory

School House

Dressmaker

Harvest Barn

Gazette Printing Office

Doctor's Home

McDiarmid Home

Crysler Home

Ross' Farm

Drag Saw

Cabinetmaker

Willard's Hotel

Providence Chapel

Bakery

Mill Pond

Workman's Home

Blacksmith

Crysler Store

Engine House

Robertson Home

Tin Shop

Broommaker

Christ Church

Pastor's Home

Beach's Saw Mill

Cook's Tavern and Livery

Bellamy's Steam Flour Mills

Asselstine's Woolen Factory

Photographer

Village Store and Post Office

Native Peoples in Ontario Area, About 1740

Imagine that you could step back in time. What would you find? Who would be living where you live now 150, 200, or even 250 years ago?

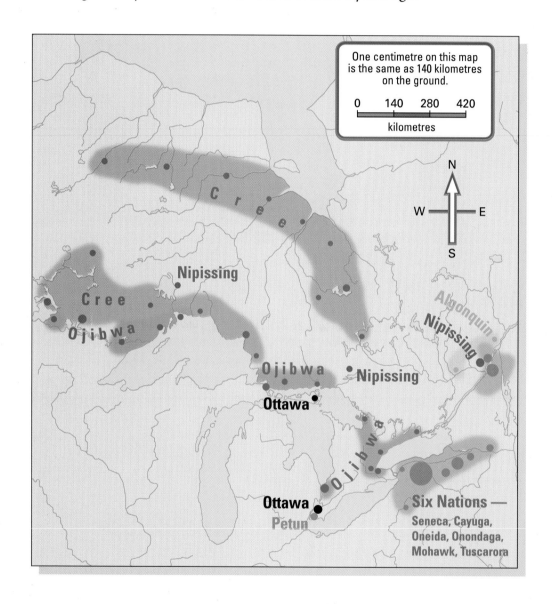

One centimetre on this map is the same as 140 kilometres on the ground.

0   140   280   420
kilometres

Cree

Nipissing

Cree

Ojibwa

Algonquin
Nipissing

Ojibwa   Nipissing

Ottawa

Ojibwa

Ottawa
Petun

Six Nations —
Seneca, Cayuga,
Oneida, Onondaga,
Mohawk, Tuscarora

Settlement in Upper Canada

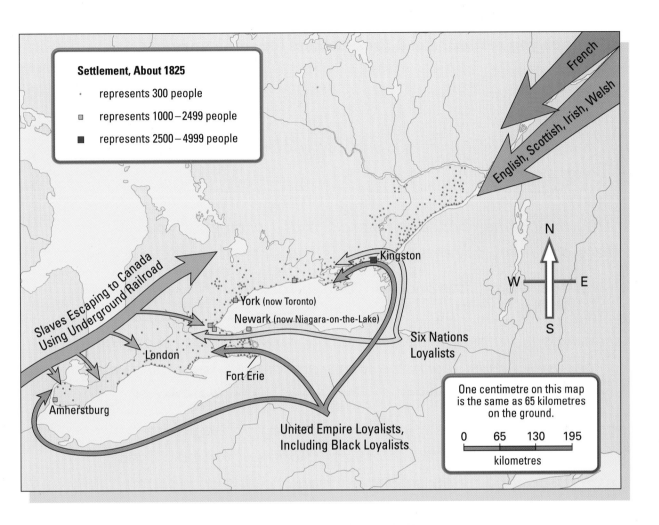

Settlement, About 1825

· represents 300 people

▫ represents 1000–2499 people

■ represents 2500–4999 people

French

English, Scottish, Irish, Welsh

Slaves Escaping to Canada Using Underground Railroad

Kingston

York (now Toronto)

Newark (now Niagara-on-the-Lake)

London

Fort Erie

Amherstburg

Six Nations Loyalists

United Empire Loyalists, Including Black Loyalists

N W E S

One centimetre on this map is the same as 65 kilometres on the ground.

0   65   130   195

kilometres

People Living in Ontario in 1851—Where They Were Born

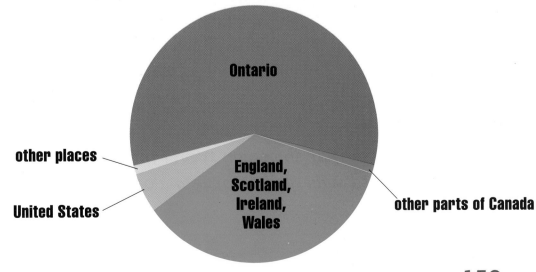

Ontario

other places

United States

England, Scotland, Ireland, Wales

other parts of Canada

To a New Life in Upper Canada

Imagine moving to Upper Canada in the 1820s. How would you get there? How long would your trip take? What would life be like once you settled? Read these letters for some answers.

June 20, 1821–Kingston

Dear Jean,

You may remember, dear sister, that I promised you letters about my adventure. Here is the first of many.

The trip from Liverpool to Québec took seven weeks' journey under sail. Dear Henry and I stayed well, but baby Karen was ill with fever. She is better now that we're off the cramped ship. I must learn the local remedies to keep her well!

From Québec we took a steamboat to Montréal. (The tide does not flow as far as Montréal and the trip would be difficult for square-rigged ships.) At Montréal we portaged— travelling on land by horse and carriage to get around the dangerous rapids. At the village of La Chine, our belongings were put onto bateaux. (These flat-bottomed boats are each rowed by five rowers, plus one man steering with a paddle.) We continued by carriage until we came to the Ottawa River. There, we took a ferry across—a raft!

Once across the Ottawa River, we travelled a good road through a beautiful oak forest. Later we passed fields of wheat, rye, Native corn, potatoes, and turnips. There are plans for a canal so that ships can travel this stretch of the St. Lawrence, but I was glad to have a close-up view of the countryside.

Our first taste of Upper Canada came at Glengarry. Most of the settlers are Scottish. One told Henry of how he arrived two years ago with next to nothing and now owns a house, three hectares of crops, cows, and sheep. We hope to do this well!

We continued by horse and carriage to the riverside villages of Prescott and Brockville. From Brockville we travelled by bateaux because the road is very bad. The winds and currents are so strong through the Thousand Islands that the La Chine-to-Kingston trip by bateaux often takes seven days.

Now we are in Kingston. I can see the war ship the <u>St. Lawrence</u>, a fort, and a dockyard. How strange to have seen so few people since Montréal and now so many again! As I write this, we are waiting for the weekly steamboat to York—the capital of Upper Canada. There we will apply for land at the Land Office.

Keep well, dear sister,
love,
Patricia

161

August 15, 1821—near Chatham

Dear Jean,

We have settled at last. The land is south of the Thames River, southwest of Chatham. (Chatham has one church and a few houses, plus building lots ready for more. The closest big town is Amherstburg, with 1000 people.) If we clear one twentieth of the land, make a road on one side of it, and build a reasonable log house, the land will truly be ours. The government will grant it to us!

Our trip here was both beautiful and distressing. From York, we went by steamboat to Newark, then Queenston. From there we portaged around the grand Niagara Falls! (They are awesome and cannot be described!) Then we travelled by steamboat, horse and carriage, and foot to our home. There is a road from the western tip of Lake Ontario to Chatham, but it's very bad in places and travels through what is called the Long Wood.

Now we combine the work of building the log house and barn AND clearing some land to plant before winter sets in.

Keep well, dear sister. I think of you often.
love,
Patricia

This reproduction from a map of Upper Canada published in 1813, shows the Chatham area.

December 28, 1821—near Chatham

Dear Jean,

Winter has changed the land and given us some quiet time. So, at last, I write you.

Our log house and barn are built. We now have a cow, two oxen, and pigs. Henry has cleared trees from some of the land, and we planted the fields with wheat. Planting now gives the crop a head start on next season. (As soon as we can grow more wheat than we need, we can sell it for export. Lower Canada wants it and we will need the money.) For now, we eat mainly pork and bread, plus milk from our cow. Joseph, a Native hunter, sold us venison when he last shot a deer nearby. We were thankful for the change!

Our log house and barn are rough, but working with neighbours to build them was a joy. We're learning so much from the people here—how to grow Native corn, rotate the crops we plant, and make maple sugar. Henry is learning from Joseph how to trap in the woods. And from Joseph's mother, Molly, I'm learning about herbal medicines and what wild plants can be eaten.

Baby Karen is well and will soon have a new brother or sister. We all send our love. Please send news of home and the family,

love,

Patricia

Herbal Remedies

Bulbs of **wild onion** made into a paste

for asthma attacks and colds, and to repel insects

garlic made into a tea, syrup, and other forms

for coughs, asthma, heart problems, and digestion

mint leaves made into a tea and other forms

for stomach aches, chest pains, and heart problems

juice of the **dandelion** root made into a tea

for the liver

inside bark of the **willow** tree chewed

for general pain relief

crushed **yarrow** leaves and other forms of yarrow

to stop blood flowing—for example, from cuts

Yarrow

Canada's Coat of Arms

Like some families, cities, and other countries, Canada has a coat of arms. It's an official symbol shaped like a shield. A coat of arms is a way of showing some things that make a group of people or a place special.

Canada's coat of arms shows symbols of England, Scotland, Ireland, and France—countries that many early settlers came from.

- The three royal lions on the shield, the lion holding the Union Jack flag, and the English roses represent England.
- Scotland is represented by the royal lion on the shield, the unicorn, and the thistles.
- Ireland is represented by the harp on the shield and the shamrocks.
- The flag of Royal France and the fleur-de-lis on the shield and at the bottom of the coat represent France.
- The maple leaves represent Canada.

The words that circle the shield mean "They desire a better country." The saying at the bottom is the official motto of Canada: "From sea to sea."

If you made a coat of arms for your family, what would you put on it? What makes your family special?

Acknowledgements

Harcourt Canada would like to thank the students from the Board of Education for the City of Windsor for their assistance in developing title pages for TAPESTRY.

Text

Islands

If Once You Have Slept on an Island: Copyright © 1926 by The Century Company. From *Taxis and Toadstools* by Rachel Field. Used by permission of Random House Children's Books, a division of Random House, Inc. Dell Books for Young Readers. **It's Cold Here But It's Fun:** Text by Penny Williams reprinted from OWL magazine with permission of the publisher, Owl Communications, Toronto. **Celia's Island Journal:** Copyright © 1992 by Loretta Krupinski. By permission of Little, Brown and Company.

Celebrations

Celebrate What? Celebrate When: Adapted from *Let's Celebrate!* by Caroline Parry used by permission of Kids Can Press, Ltd., Toronto. Text copyright © 1987 by Caroline Parry. "The New Suit" by Nidia S. de Romero. Reprinted with permission of the poet. **Celebrating in a Cold Place:** Adapted from "It's Cold Here, But It's Fun!" Text by Penny Williams reprinted from OWL magazine with permission of the publisher, Owl Communications Inc., Toronto. **Tree of Cranes:** Adapted from *Tree of Cranes*. Copyright © 1991 by Allen Say. Reprinted by permission of Houghton Mifflin Company. All rights reserved.

Generations

I Love the Moon, the Stars, and the Ancestors: From *This Land is my Land* by George Littlechild. Reprinted with permission of Children's Book Press. **The Always Prayer Shawl:** Adapted from *The Always Prayer Shawl* by Sheldon Oberman. Published by Boyds Mills Press. Reprinted with permission of the publisher.

Illustrations

Islands

Sarah Jane English: p. 7; **Hon Leong** (custom logotype): p. 7; **Heather Graham:** pp. 8–9, 54; **Sami Suomalinen:** p. 11; **Deborah Crowle** (maps): pp. 12–13, 30, 38–40, 45; **Dorothy Siemens:** pp. 15, 49; **Carl Wiens:** pp. 16–17; **Leon Zernitsky:** pp. 24–28, 48, 50–51; **John Fraser:** p. 29; **Malcolm Cullen:** pp. 46–47.

Celebrations

Hon Leong (custom logotype): p. 55; **Steven Taylor:** pp. 56–57; **Dorothy Siemens:** pp. 63, 71, 84, 85, 91; **Patty Gallinger:** p. 63; **Deborah Crowle (maps):** pp. 68–70, 74–75, 89–90, 94; **Henry Van der Linde:** pp. 71, 73; **Eric Copeland:** pp. 74–75; **John Fraser:** p. 77; **Anson Liaw:** p. 80; **Don Kilby:** p. 84; **Susan Todd:** pp. 92–93; **Kathryn Adams:** p. 102.

Generations

Greg Douglas: p. 103; **Hon Leung** (custom logotype): p. 103; **Henry Van der Linde:** pp. 104, 130–131; **Deborah Crowle** (map): p. 115; **June Lawrason:** 120–123; **Drew-Brook-Cormack:** pp. 124–127; **Don Kilby:** pp. 128–129; **Megan Byrne:** 132–133; **Suzanne Mogensen:** pp. 136–138; **Eric Copeland:** 141–143.

Information Station

Deborah Crowle (maps): pp. 152-53, 157-159, 163; **William Kimber:** p. 161; **Dorothy Siemens:** p. 165.

Photographs

Islands

p. 12: © Al Harvey; **p. 13 (top):** © P.G. Adam/Publiphoto; **p. 13 (centre):** © Marilynn McAra; **p. 13 (bottom):** © Jack Maclean; **p. 18 (both):** © Al Harvey; **pp. 19-20:** © Chris Cheadle; **p. 21:** © David Neel; **pp. 22-23:** © Paul Fletcher; **p. 24:** © Marine Atlantic; **pp. 27-28:** © Camera Art; **p. 31:** © Fred Bruemmer; **p. 32:** © Tessa MacIntosh/ NWT Archives; **p. 33:** © Jerry Apanasowicz; **p. 34:** © 1996, Comstock; **p. 36 (top):** © V.C. Last/ Geographical Visual Aids; **p. 36 (centre):** © V.C. Last/Geographical Visual Aids; **p. 36 (bottom):** © Claye Explorer/Publiphoto; **p. 37:** © McCutcheon/Visuals Unlimited; **p. 41 (top):** © Airphoto Intl. Ltd/Altitude/Publiphoto; **p. 41 (centre):** © K. Straiton/Publiphoto; **p. 42 (bottom):** © Al Harvey; **p. 42 (top):** © Al Harvey; **p. 42 (centre):** © Bart Barlow/Envision; **p. 43 (top):** © Paparazzi/Publiphoto; **p. 43 (centre):** © Chuck O'Rear/Woodfin Camp & Associates; **p. 43 (bottom):** © Kal Muller/Woodfin Camp & Associates; **p. 52 (top):** © P. Baeza/Publiphoto; **p. 52 (centre right):** © Explorer/Publiphoto; **p. 52 (centre left):** © C. Girouard/Publiphoto; **p. 52 (bottom):** © Beedell/Canada in Stock.